Spelling Success

CLASS 5

Peter Clutterbuck

Blake
EDUCATION
Better ways to learn

To Jessie O'Brien

Spelling Success Class 5

Published by Scholastic India Pvt. Ltd.
A-27, Ground Floor, Sigma Centre
Infocity-1, Sector 34, Gurgaon-122001 (India)
Info-in@scholastic.asia

Author: Peter Clutterbuck
Editor: Kerry Davies
Cover and internal design: Janice Bowles
Typesetter: Julian Mole, Post Pre Press.

ISBN: 978-93-5471-896-0
First edition 2010
This reprint edition: June 2024
Printed in India

Contents

Term 1

Term 2

Contents continued

Term 3

✓ Tick when completed

Term 4

✓ Tick when completed

Appendixes

About This Book

The *Spelling Success* series provides students with learning activities that embrace the different elements of the spelling system. Each book focuses on the different scope and sequences in the development of spelling skills for each age group or skill level.

These books are not a complete spelling course in themselves, neither are they meant to be, but they provide both students and teachers with the content needed to produce best practices in spelling.

The activities in each book are sequential through the four terms of the school year. This means that it's best to start at the beginning of the Term 1 section and work though to the end, before commencing Term 2 activities, and so on. There are 76 units in this book, 18 per term plus four Review and Test units. Each term is divided into the four areas of knowledge that need to be understood and learned in order to develop a comprehensive mastery of spelling:

Phonological Knowledge — how words sound

Word Function Knowledge — how word function can change spelling

Meaning Knowledge — how context can change word form

Word History Knowledge — how words have been derived

The Phonological Knowledge and the Word Function Knowledge sections include Revision and Test sheets for each term. Four units of Review and Test sheets covering the whole book are provided at the end of Term 4.

This book also contains useful tools to support students with their spelling. At the back of the book you'll find:

- ★ Useful Words list
- ★ WINK: Words I Need to Know — space to record problematic words
- ★ Some Tips for Learning to Spell
- ★ Assessment checklist
- ★ Glossary of Terms

Answers to all activities are provided in a special liftout section. A useful **topic list** for the whole year is given before the units.

Spelling Success provides an integrated method of teaching phonics, spelling and vocabulary. These books will improve literacy skills through effective instruction and evaluation based on the latest research into how spelling is best taught and learned successfully.

Book 5 Topic Chart

Vowel sounds, a

A The letter a is sometimes pronounced as a short **a** sound, as in **bat** and **apple**. Find the words in the grid and write them beside their meanings below.

d	r	a	g	o	n	m
a	c	g	n	a	t	a
m	a	t	a	x	i	t
n	m	a	p	p	l	e
a	e	f	l	a	s	h
l	l	l	a	m	b	s

1. baby sheep ________________
2. small biting insect ________________
3. animal with a hump ________________
4. fruit ________________
5. mythical fire-breathing creature ________________
6. water reservoir ________________
7. car for hire ________________
8. sudden bright light ________________
9. floor covering ________________

B Sometimes the letter **a** is a long **a** sound, as in **male** and **cradle**. Write each word from the box beside its meaning below.

whale	**stable**	**crane**	**strange**
paste	**chase**	**exhale**	**oasis**

1. bird ________________
2. to go after ________________
3. odd ________________
4. glue ________________
5. horses' home ________________
6. breathe out ________________
7. fertile spot in a desert ________________
8. large ocean mammal ________________

C The letter **a** can also make an **ar** sound, as in **last**, or a short **o** sound, as in **wallow**. Write the words from the box under their correct headings below.

brass swamp swallow telecast squash flask koala quarrel

a = ar sound		**a = o sound**	
________________	________________	________________	________________
________________	________________	________________	________________

Parent/Teacher Signature   Date

UNIT 2

Vowel sounds, e

A The letter **e** can be a short **e** sound, as in **bent** and **sent**. The words in the box have been cramped together. Find them and write each one beside its meaning below.

insectscentleveldentistfleshshedfreshfencerentdresscentseven

1. ladies' clothing ____________
2. person who cares for teeth ____________
3. new, not stale ____________
4. money paid to lease a home ____________
5. border to keep in cattle ____________
6. small creature with six legs ____________
7. money ____________
8. odour, smell ____________
9. meat ____________
10. farm building ____________
11. number ____________
12. even ____________

B Sometimes the letter **e** makes a long **e** sound, where the final **e** makes the middle **e** say its name, as in **these** and **concrete**. Write each word from the box in the correct sentence below.

recede
serene
concrete
sincere
atmosphere
complete
severe
athlete
sphere
stampede

1. I am sure his apology was ____________.
2. The missile zoomed through the Earth's ____________.
3. The buffalo began to ____________ with the sudden noise.
4. At last the jigsaw puzzle is ____________.
5. Joshua has a ____________ cold and will not be at school.
6. Oliver is worried as his hairline is beginning to ____________.
7. The footpath is made of ____________.
8. The Earth is the shape of a ____________.
9. Mia is a keen ____________ and may go to the Olympics one day.
10. The sleeping children made the room peaceful and ____________.

Parent/Teacher Signature Date

Vowel sounds, i

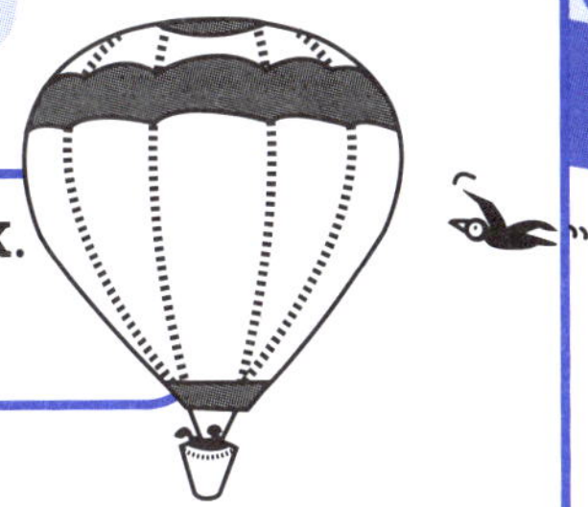

A The letter **i** can be a short **i** sound, as in **fix** and **trick**.
Write each word from the box in the correct space.

comic
hospital
limb
picnic
tickle
litter
sister
thistle
prison
liquid

1. The sharp _____________ hurt my finger.
2. My _____________ works as a nurse at the hospital.
3. There was a disappointing amount of _____________ on the road.
4. The injured person was rushed to the _________________.
5. I really enjoyed reading that funny _____________.
6. The criminal will be in this _____________ for ten more years.
7. If you _____________ me under the armpits I will laugh.
8. Water and oil are both kinds of _____________.
9. Yesterday we went on a _____________ in the bush.
10. Jack's heavy weight caused the _____________ of the tree to break.

B Sometimes the letter **i** is a long **i** sound, where the final **e** makes the **i** say its name, as in **fine** and **mine**.
The words in the box have been cramped up. Find each word and write it beside its meaning below.

hostilehivefragilespidervampirestridesciencewinerequirepolitefertilemo-bile

1. eight-legged creature _____________
2. school subject _____________
3. courteous, not rude _____________
4. movable _____________
5. angry, belligerent _____________
6. bees' home _____________
7. easily broken _____________
8. long step _____________
9. drink made from grapes _____________
10. need _____________
11. rich soil _____________
12. blood-sucking bat _____________

Parent/Teacher Signature Date

UNIT 4

Vowel sounds, o

A The letter o can be a short o sound, as in **box** and **stop**.
Write each short o word from the box in the correct sentence.

compost
lollipop
shock
continent
bottle
wombat
foxes
broth

1. The small boy enjoyed sucking the sweet ________________.
2. Asia is the largest ________________.
3. Australia has many feral ________________.
4. He brought a ________________ of water to school to drink.
5. The ________________ was captured in its burrow.
6. We had only a light ________________ for lunch as we were dieting.
7. The ________________ of the news made him faint.
8. The gardener used the ________________ to fertilse his garden.

B Sometimes the letter o is a long o sound, as in **toe** and **flow**.
Write each word from the box beside a word it can be linked to.

doze	**hose**	**toe**	**hotel**
cone	**stone**	**throne**	**frozen**

1. sleep ________________
2. ice-cream ________________
3. rock ________________
4. king ________________
5. ice ________________
6. inn ________________
7. foot ________________
8. water ________________

C The words in the box have either short or long o sounds, or the o is pronounced as a short u sound, as in **done**. Write the words under the correct headings below.

cove	**among**	**lodge**	**sponge**	**lonely**	**content**

o = short o sound	**o = long o sound**	**o = short u sound**
________________	________________	________________
________________	________________	________________

Parent/Teacher Signature Date

Vowel sounds, u

A The letter u can be a short u sound, as in **cut** and **but**. Write each word from the box beside a word it can be linked to in some way.

adult	**sunrise**	**crumb**	**slum**	**hundred**	**ugly**
skunk	**trunk**	**umbrella**	**drudge**	**uncle**	**under**

1. bread ____________
2. elephant ____________
3. hovel ____________
4. dawn ____________
5. auntie ____________
6. child ____________
7. rain ____________
8. work ____________
9. duckling ____________
10. century ____________
11. above ____________
12. smell ____________

B Sometimes u makes a long u sound, where the final e makes u say its name, as in **cute** and **reduce**.
Write each word from the box beside its meaning below.

amuse	**bugle**	**confuse**	**furniture**	**puncture**	**duel**
pupil	**moisture**	**secure**	**future**	**perfume**	**population**

1. dampness ____________
2. muddle up ____________
3. tables, chairs ____________
4. fight between two ____________
5. part of the eye ____________
6. number of people ____________
7. entertain ____________
8. safe ____________
9. ahead of time ____________
10. musical instrument ____________
11. flat tyre ____________
12. scent ____________

Parent/Teacher Signature Date

Sound patterns, ar, ai and ay

A The letters **ar** are often pronounced as in **car** and **star**.
Write each word from the box in its correct sentence.

burglar **vinegar** **sugar** **separate** **marble** **carpet** **cigar** **depart** **carve** **orchard**

1. I used two spoonfuls of ______________ to sweeten my tea.
2. The wealthy man smoked a fat ______________.
3. What time do you hope to ______________ from here?
4. Dad was angry when Riley spilled the paint on the ______________.
5. My brother asked if he could ______________ the roast for dinner.
6. The ______________ was soon arrested by the police.
7. We sprinkled ______________ over our fish and chips.
8. Lots of apricot trees grow in the ______________.
9. The statue has been carved from a piece of white ______________.
10. It took us a long time to ______________ the fighting boys.

B The letters **ai** and **ay** are often pronounced as a long **a** sound, as in **rain** and **way**.
Look at the words in the box. Each contains either **ai** or **ay**, pronounced as a long **a** sound. Write each beside a word it can be linked to in some way.

play	**daisy**	**tray**	**quail**	**remain**	**hurray**
rainbow	**container**	**holiday**	**faithful**	**bait**	**straight**

1. bottle ______________
2. dog ______________
3. fishing ______________
4. cheer ______________
5. bent ______________
6. bird ______________
7. platter ______________
8. petal ______________
9. sport ______________
10. spectrum ______________
11. beach ______________
12. stay ______________

Parent/Teacher Signature Date

Revision

A Write the words in the box under the correct headings below.

brake	elastic	tasty	bacon	dragon	exhale
debate	taxi	animal	gravel	apricot	bandit

Short a sound ____________ ____________ ____________ ____________ ____________ ____________

Long a sound ____________ ____________ ____________ ____________ ____________ ____________

B Sort the words in the box under the correct headings below.

vent	invert	compete	swept
female	knit	ledge	skill
fetch	athlete	until	brine
polite	whine	shrine	concrete

Short e sound	Long e sound	Short i sound	Long i sound
____________	____________	____________	____________
____________	____________	____________	____________
____________	____________	____________	____________
____________	____________	____________	____________

C Add the sound units **ai** = long **a** sound, **ar** = **ar** sound or **ay** = long **a** sound in the blanks below.

1. I travelled through the subw_____.
2. I had a tight belt around my w_____st.
3. The ship carried lots of c_____go.
4. The priest pr_____ed for the child.
5. We kept the qu_____l in the aviary.
6. He wore a blue c_____digan to school.

Parent/Teacher Signature Date

UNIT 8

Test 1

The underlined words are spelled incorrectly. Write each word correctly in the space.

1	At the zoo we saw a <u>camal</u> with two humps.	1
2	The statue is made of <u>marbel</u>.	2
3	The old dog was loyal and <u>faythfull</u>.	3
4	The <u>skunck</u> frightened the dog away with its smell.	4
5	The lady wore a sweet-smelling <u>purfume</u> to the party.	5
6	In the army Joseph plays the <u>bugel</u>.	6
7	The <u>spida</u> made a web in the roof.	7
8	This <u>bottel</u> is made of glass.	8
9	We stayed the night in the city <u>hottel</u>.	9
10	The explorer studied the land through a <u>teleskope</u>.	10
11	This brick is made of <u>concrite</u>.	11
12	The sick girl was taken to the <u>horspital</u>.	12

Total correct ______ / 12

Parent/Teacher Signature   Date

Test 2

Choose the correct spelling from the words in brackets and write it in the space.

1	We saw a (wale, wail, whale) in the ocean.	1
2	A (kanal, canal, canel) is a type of artifical watercourse.	2
3	A (swallow, swollow, swaller) is a small bird.	3
4	My mother went to the (dentist, dentst, dentest).	4
5	Tom the (athaleet, athlete, athleet) won every race.	5
6	We went for a (picnic, piknic, picknik) in the park.	6
7	My favourite school subject is (sience, siance, science).	7
8	I spent all my (money, monee, muni) at the show.	8
9	The water in the pipe is (frozin, frozan, frozen).	9
10	I took an (umberella, umbrella, umrella) in case of rain.	10
11	The car has a (punchure, puncture, puntcher).	11
12	The (burglar, burgular, burgla) was caught by police.	12

Total correct ______ / 12

Parent/Teacher Signature Date

Plurals, adding s or es

Plural means more than one. Nouns form their plurals in a number of ways:

★ By simply adding **s** to the end of the word. Examples: one book, two books; one tree, seven trees

★ By adding es to nouns that end in **ch**, **s**, **sh**, **ss** or **x**. Examples: one match, a box of matches; one bus, three buses; one glass, a tray of glasses; one marsh, many marshes; one box, a dozen boxes

In the blanks, write the correct plural of the noun given in the brackets at the end of each sentence.

1. Six _______________ in the street were damaged by the fire. (house)
2. She sewed three _______________ in her torn dress. (patch)
3. We washed the _______________ and then dried them all. (dish)
4. Charlotte brings lots of _______________ to school. (pencil)
5. We drew _______________ in our books for Halloween. (witch)
6. Many _______________ have occurred at this crossroads. (crash)
7. Chloe always seems to have plenty of new _______________ to wear. (dress)
8. The four school _______________ are in the parking lot. (bus)
9. The convict was given ten _______________ of the cat-o'-nine-tails. (lash)
10. We stacked six _______________ on the table. (box)
11. The experienced boxer landed many painful _______________ on his opponent. (punch)
12. Several _______________ are away at camp today. (class)
13. The loving mother gave her baby many _______________. (kiss)
14. Australia has many beautiful sandy _______________. (beach)
15. We had to listen to a number of boring _______________. (speech)
16. During the cricket match Billy took several _______________. (catch)

Parent/Teacher Signature Date

Plurals, words ending in y

Plural means more than one. Nouns form their plurals in a number of ways:

★ Some nouns that end in **y** after a vowel form their plurals simply by adding **s**.
Example: one key, two keys

★ For nouns that end in **y** after a consonant, drop the **y**, replace it with an **i** and then add **es**.
Example: one poppy, two poppies

Write the plural of each noun given in the brackets at the end of each sentence.

1. There are five ________________ on the table. (lolly)
2. The two young ________________ galloped across the paddock. (filly)
3. There are several narrow ________________ in this part of the city. (alley)
4. At the farm we saw lots of ________________. (donkey)
5. The ________________ began to mount their horses before the race. (jockey)
6. There are three different ________________ for us to eat. (jelly)
7. All the ________________ here make it difficult to enjoy the food. (fly)
8. Our teacher has many ________________ at the moment. (worry)
9. We took the four ________________ back to the supermarket. (trolley)
10. The ________________ in this forest all go in different directions. (pathway)
11. Switzerland is a country with many high mountains and deep ________________. (valley)
12. We have several ________________ to observe special times. (holiday)
13. This house has two ________________. (chimney)
14. The ________________ of the workers cost many millions of dollars. (salary)
15. Every student in my class has two ________________. (diary)
16. There are lots of large ________________ in our city. (factory)

Parent/Teacher Signature Date

UNIT 12

Plurals, words ending in f, fe or o

Plural means more than one. Nouns form their plurals in a number of ways:

★ For most nouns that end in **f** or **fe**, you change the **f** to **v** and add **es**. Examples: one leaf, two leaves; one knife, a set of knives. However, some simply add **s**. Examples: one chief, two chiefs; one giraffe, a herd of giraffes

★ Most nouns that end in **o** also add **es** to become plural. Example: one potato, six potatoes. However, some simply add **s**. Example: one piano, two pianos

Add the correct form of the noun given in the bracket at the end of each sentence.

1. I read the story about Snow White and the Seven ________________. (dwarf)
2. There are several ________________ in the zoo. (giraffe)
3. The two ________________ I wore kept me warm. (scarf)
4. We cut all the ________________ into chips. (potato)
5. There are many ________________ in Australian history. (hero)
6. The two ________________ of bread were placed on the table. (loaf)
7. There were several ________________ of pumpkins left on the table. (half)
8. The five ________________ kept chasing the injured deer. (wolf)
9. My cold was so bad I used three ________________________ during lunchtime. (handkerchief)
10. Our school has four ________________. (piano)
11. The children decided to help them________________ to the food. (self)
12. These five sharp ________________ are on the table. (knife)
13. We read about the ________________ of the explorers. (life)
14. We could hear many ______________ from the mountaineers. (echo)
15. Destructive ____________________ swept across the land. (tornado)
16. We stacked the groceries on the four ________________. (shelf)

Parent/Teacher Signature Date

Plurals, complete change or none

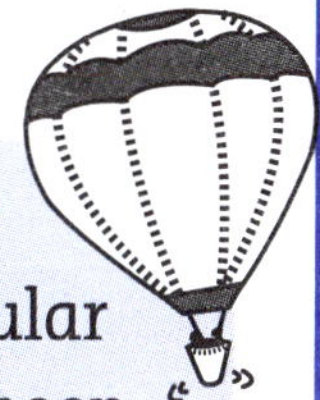

Plural means more than one. Nouns form their plurals in a number of ways:

★ Some nouns make their plurals by completely changing their structure.
Example: one mouse, two mice

★ Some nouns have only one word to indicate both singular and plural. Example: one sheep, a flock of sheep

★ Some nouns have no singular form at all. Example: jeans

In the blanks, write the plural of each noun given in brackets at the end of the sentences. Remember some will not change and some will have a total change.

1. There were six ________________ in the field. (deer)
2. He wore long ________________ to the party instead of shorts. (trousers)
3. The ______________ were well behaved all day. (child)
4. There are lots of ________________ in the pantry. (mouse)
5. His two front ________________ were damaged in the accident. (tooth)
6. We caught seven ________________ in the river. (trout)
7. Ned Kelly was hanged on the ________________. (gallows)
8. The blacksmith used the ________________ to flame the fire. (bellows)
9. She used the _______________ to cut the paper. (scissors)
10. There are many ________________ in the room. (woman)
11. There were a lot of ________________ in the paddock. (cattle)
12. Both ________________ are quite sore. (foot).
13. There are a number of ________________ of this insect. (species)
14. Our teacher cannot find her new ________________. (spectacles)
15. She removed all the _______________ from her hair. (louse)
16. There are many ________________ on this farm. (goose)

Parent/Teacher Signature Date

UNIT 14

Revision

A Find each word in the grid and write it on the line in the first column. Beside each word write its plural form in the second column.

j	e	l	l	y	f	l	y
e	n	g	i	n	e	l	b
s	t	i	t	c	h	o	o
m	o	n	k	e	y	a	d
k	i	d	n	e	y	f	y
e	c	h	o	f	o	o	t

1. ______________ ______________
2. ______________ ______________
3. ______________ ______________
4. ______________ ______________
5. ______________ ______________
6. ______________ ______________
7. ______________ ______________
8. ______________ ______________
9. ______________ ______________
10. ______________ ______________

B Circle the correct plural word in the brackets.

1. There are lots of (mouses, mice) in the house.
2. This building is ten (storeys, stories) high.
3. The prince has had several (wifes, wives).
4. I ate the ten juicy (berrys, berries).
5. The mother gave the baby lots of (kises, kisses).
6. I dropped the three (saucas, saucers) and they broke.
7. We have played six (matches, matchs) this year.
8. There are ten (busses, buses) in the carpark.
9. There are some large (citys, cities) in Australia.
10. She gave me both of the sharp (knifes, knives).

Parent/Teacher Signature Date

Test

The underlined word in each sentence is incorrect. Write the correct word in the box.

	Sentence	Answer
1	Olivia has over twenty <u>pencillss</u>.	1
2	The baby girl gave her mother lots of <u>kises</u>.	2
3	Our class has lots of <u>diarys</u>.	3
4	There are many large <u>factorys</u> in our town.	4
5	The <u>jockies</u> all began to mount the horses.	5
6	There are lots of <u>mouses</u> in the kitchen.	6
7	The six sharp <u>knifes</u> were kept in the drawer.	7
8	We put the cans of food on the three <u>shelfs</u>.	8
9	Our house has two valuable <u>pianoes</u>.	9
10	We picked all the <u>tomatos</u> from the bush.	10
11	This building is six <u>stories</u> high.	11
12	I used six <u>matchs</u> to light the fire.	12

Total correct ______ / 12

Parent/Teacher Signature Date

UNIT 16

Homophones 1

Homophones are a type of word called a homonym. They are words that sound the same but have different spellings and different meanings.

Examples: bear (to carry, or a type of animal) and bare (barren or naked)

Choose the correct word in the brackets. Write it in the spaces.

1. Smoking is (band, banned) in this café. ______________
2. We had apple strudel for our (desert, dessert). ______________
3. The powerful (currant, current) swept the swimmers away. ______________
4. We watch a TV (serial, cereal) each night. ______________
5. We put tomato (source, sauce) on our pies. ______________
6. The bolt of (lightning, lightening) struck the tall tower. ______________
7. We allowed the (guest, guessed) to use the main bedroom. ______________
8. The (hire, higher) branches of the tree must be cut down. ______________
9. We tried to (hire, higher) a front-end loader. ______________
10. The (band, banned) played lots of songs I enjoy. ______________
11. We are (lightning, lightening) the load to make it easier to lift. ______________
12. The (desert, dessert) areas of Australia are extremely arid. ______________
13. I found a red (currant, current) in my cake. ______________
14. We could not locate the (source, sauce) of the strange noise. ______________
15. It took me a while before I (guest, guessed) the answer. ______________
16. I ate some (serial, cereal) for breakfast. ______________

Parent/Teacher Signature Date

Homophones 2

Homophones are words that sound the same but have different spellings and different meanings. Examples: see (to have sight) and sea (body of water)

Look closely at the pairs of homophones in the box. Write each in the correct sentence.

root	route	night	knight	border	boarder	pedal	peddle
bury	berry	hanger	hangar	miner	minor	censor	sensor

1. The bicycle ________________ squeaked as it moved.
2. The aeroplane was stored in the ________________.
3. They took a long ________________ on sidetracks to get to the city.
4. The dog is trying to ________________ the bone in the backyard.
5. It will be a bright moonlit ________________ soon.
6. The new ________________ asked if he could have a shower each morning.
7. The ________________ decided to cut the offending words from the story.
8. There was an accident at the crossroads but it was only ________________.
9. Riley works as a ________________ in a Tasmanian goldmine.
10. The Murray River forms the ________________ between two states.
11. The ________________ displayed his coat of arms proudly on this shield.
12. The ________________ of the plant soon took up the moisture.
13. I ate the juicy ________________ we found on the tree.
14. I used a coat ________________ to hold my shirts.
15. A pedlar was a person who would ________________ goods to country people.
16. The ________________ light soon picked up the movement of the burglar.

Parent/Teacher Signature Date

UNIT 18

Root words

Each of the following sentences has a missing word that is derived from the root word given in the brackets, along with its meaning.

Write a word in each of the spaces that is suitable for the meaning of the sentence.

1. I used a ____________________ glass to study the insect. (magnus = great)
2. The strong ____________________ swept the swimmers away. (curro = I run)
3. The path of the car driven by the drunk man was quite ____________________. (erro = I wander)
4. The large ____________________ clapped loudly. (audio = I hear)
5. The priest stood behind the ____________________. (altus = high)
6. The ____________________ was fired from the submarine. (mitto = I send)
7. The surgeon performed the delicate ____________________. (opus = work)
8. My little sister started ____________________ school this year. (primus = first)
9. Yesterday I met a person who was an ____________________. (aster = star)
10. The famous film star gave me her ____________________. (grapho = I write)
11. This machine runs by ____________________. (elektrom = amber)
12. The firefighters connected the hose to the street ____________________. (hydor = water)
13. She uses a lot of ____________________ to beautify herself. (kosmos = beauty)
14. The ____________________ on the bicycle became loose. (pes or pedis = foot)
15. He read a book about the ____________________ of ancient peoples. (lego = I read)
16. The Crusaders built a ____________________ in the mountains. (fortis = strong)
17. The farmer lived in a large house called the ____________________. (stede = place)
18. The jeweller ____________________ my name on the bracelet. (grafan = dig)

Parent/Teacher Signature Date

Sound patterns, au and aw

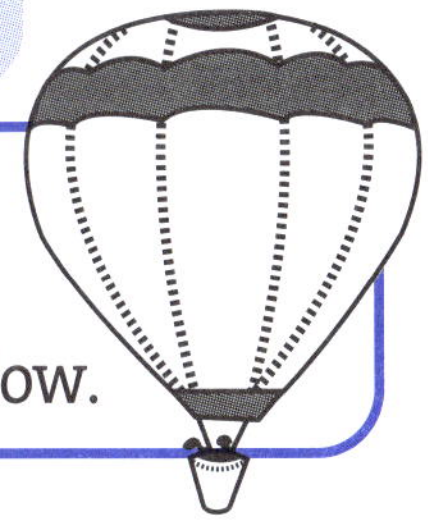

A The letters au can represent two sounds:
(a) or, as in **sauce** (b) short o, as in **sausage**.
Write the correct word from the box in each space below.

exhaust
saucer
taut
fraud
autumn
applause
automatic
auction
cauliflower
sausage

1. There was a lot of ______________ for her fine performance.
2. The gears on this new car are ______________ not manual.
3. The coloured leaves fell from the trees in ______________.
4. The ______________ on this old car makes it noisy.
5. The boys pulled the string ______________ to keep it tight.
6. The people who gave money found out later it was a ______________.
7. The cup and its ______________ are on the table.
8. I fried the ______________ in the frypan.
9. The house was sold at an ______________ last Saturday.
10. We boiled the ______________________ to eat with our meat.

B The letters aw are pronounced as in **paw** and **claw**.
Write the correct word from the box in the blank in each of the sentences.

awesome
awkward
drawl
gnaw
outlaw
scrawl
sprawled
trawler
strawberries
flaw

1. There is a small ______________ in each of these new notes.
2. When some American people speak they are said to __________.
3. Jesse James was an ____________ in the American wild west.
4. When the boy was exhausted he ______________ over the bed.
5. The tall youngster is clumsy and quite ______________.
6. The mouse began to ___________ at the cardboard box it was in.
7. The ______________ hauled up its nets full of sardines.
8. We poured rich cream all over the ______________________.
9. His writing is not much more than an untidy ______________.
10. I can only describe his great performance as ______________.

Parent/Teacher Signature Date

UNIT 20

Sound patterns, ea

The sound pattern **ea** can represent three sounds: (a) long **e**, as in **beat** and **meat** (b) long **a**, as in **break** and **steak** (c) short **e**, as in **head** or **bread**.

A Find each **ea** word in the box, and write it in the correct sentence. They are all long **e** sounds.

s	e	a	s	o	n	b	g
b	l	e	a	c	h	e	r
t	r	e	a	t	y	a	e
s	q	u	e	a	k	k	a
d	i	s	e	a	s	e	s
b	r	e	a	t	h	e	e
t	e	a	c	h	e	r	s
p	e	a	c	e	f	u	l

1. Cancer is a serious ______________.
2. Our ______________ help us if we word hard.
3. My favourite ______________ of the year is summer.
4. The mechanic smothered the cogs in ______________.
5. The girls decided to ______________ their hair.
6. The dense smoke made it hard to ______________.
7. The two warring armies signed a ______________.
8. The bird used its ______________ to open the shell.
9. The mouse began to ______________ when it was caught.
10. It is quite ______________ living in the country.

B Write each **ea** word in the box beside a word below that it can be linked to in some way. These words have either long **a** or short **e** sounds.

heavy	**weapon**	**death**	**steak**	**weather**
jealousy	**break**	**dread**	**head**	**sweat**

1. gun ______________
2. envy ______________
3. weight ______________
4. smash ______________
5. grave ______________
6. meat ______________
7. climate ______________
8. perspiration ______________
9. neck ______________
10. fear ______________

Parent/Teacher Signature Date

Sound patterns, ee and oa

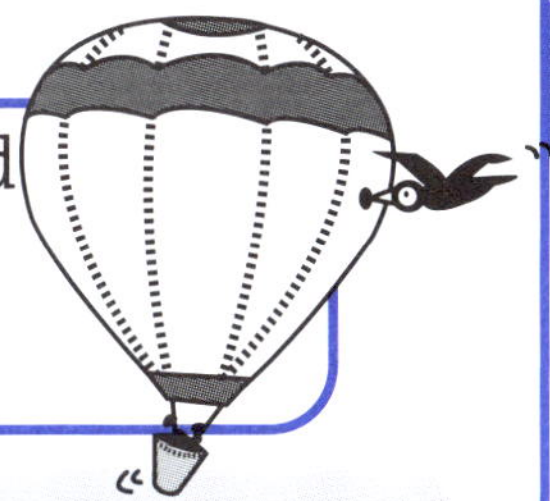

A The letters **ee** are pronounced as a long **e**, as in **feet** and **sleep**. The **ee** words in the box have been cramped up. Write each beside its meaning below.

keelbreezesucceedtoffeesneezecanteenscreechheedsteeplerefereeleechcheerful

1. to be successful ______________
2. place to get a meal ______________
3. to yell loudly ______________
4. part of a ship ______________
5. light wind ______________
6. happy, carefree ______________
7. part of a church ______________
8. umpire ______________
9. hard sweet ______________
10. blood-sucking creature ______________
11. to take notice of ______________
12. involuntary cough ______________

B The sound pattern **oa** is pronounced as a long **o** sound, as in **boat** and **coat**. Write each word in the box in its correct sentence.

approach
cocoa
soaking
toadstool
moat
loathe
loaves
hoax
coax
boastful
cloak
foam

1. I really ______________ having to clean up my room.
2. The baker gave away the ______________ of bread to a charity.
3. Around the castle was a deep ______________.
4. I tried to ______________ the horse into the float.
5. There was a lot of ______________ in the glass of beer.
6. The pilot said we would ______________ the airport shortly.
7. I had a warm cup of ______________ for supper.
8. Ethan is a very ______________ boy, always talking about himself.
9. The visitor wore a long ______________ to the dance.
10. When the water pipe burst he got a real ______________.
11. We tried not to mix up the ______________ with the mushroom.
12. The people believed them, but then realised it was a ______________.

Parent/Teacher Signature Date

Sound patterns, oo and oi

A The letters **oo** are often pronounced as a long **oo** sound, as in **boot** and **scooter**.
Write each **oo** word from the box beside its meaning below.

igloo	**noose**	**lagoon**	**bamboo**	**cockatoo**	**oozing**
hooligan	**stoop**	**kangaroo**	**cartoon**	**choosing**	**schooner**

1. large sailing ship ________________
2. hopping marsupial ________________
3. to bend down ________________
4. unruly person ________________
5. knot in a rope ________________
6. long tall grass ________________
7. Australian parrot ________________
8. seeping ________________
9. selecting ________________
10. animated movie ________________
11. home made of ice ________________
12. pool of water ________________

B The letters **oi** are usually pronounced as **oy**, as in **toil** and **foil**.
Write the **oi** words from the box in their correct sentences.

poise
poisonous
noisy
appoint
disappoint
rejoice
moisture
ointment
coin
quoit
voice
boil

1. When the water got very hot it began to ________________.
2. It was very ______________ at the disco with the loud music .
3. I hate to ________________ you but I will not be helping.
4. The team began to ______________ when they won the match.
5. We dried the cloth to rid it of any ________________.
6. They will ________________ Chloe as school captain.
7. Sally displayed grace and ______________ at the award night.
8. Do not touch those leaves as they are ____________________.
9. Joshua threw the ________________ over the base stick.
10. Because of his sore throat Jack's ________________ was quite hoarse.
11. Ella rubbed the ________________ over the bruise on her arm.
12. A cent is a small ________________.

Parent/Teacher Signature Date

Sound patterns, or and ow

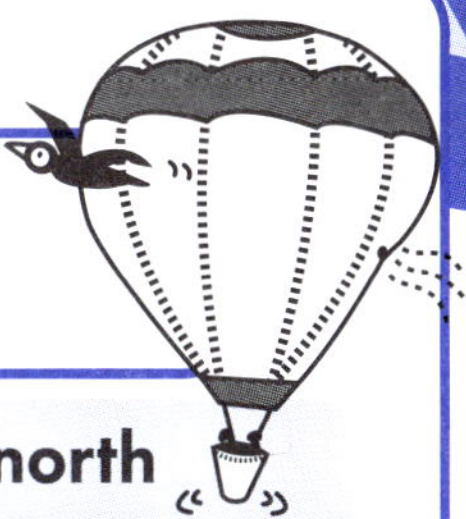

A The letters **or** are often pronounced as a long **or** sound, as in **for** and **port**. Write each **or** word beside its meaning.

enormous	**morsel**	**gorgeous**	**sword**	**orchard**	**north**
organ	**hornet**	**scorch**	**tornado**	**absorb**	**porch**

1. large wasp ________________
2. to burn ________________
3. huge ________________
4. pretty to look at ________________
5. soak up ________________
6. strong wind ________________
7. verandah ________________
8. direction ________________
9. musical instrument ________________
10. small scrap of food ________________
11. metal weapon ________________
12. farm of fruit trees ________________

B The letters **ow** are sometimes pronounced as in **how** and **fowl**. Write each **ow** word from the box beside a word it can be linked to below.

coward	**powder**	**eyebrows**	**drowsy**	**rowdy**
town	**vowel**	**trowel**	**renown**	**jowls**

1. sleepy ________________
2. village ________________
3. noisy ________________
4. hero ________________
5. talc ________________
6. consonant ________________
7. concrete ________________
8. eyelashes ________________
9. fame ________________
10. jaw ________________

C Sometimes the letters **ow** make a long **o** sound, as in **low** and **grow**. Write each word from the box in its correct sentence.

rainbow
sparrow
shallow
burrow
elbow

1. The rabbit ran down its ________________.
2. A large ________________ appeared through the cloud.
3. He hurt his ________________ when he fell on the ground.
4. That water is deep but this is ________________.
5. The ________________ built its nest in the tree.

Parent/Teacher Signature Date

Sound patterns, ou and ur

A The letters **ou** can make different sounds. Three of these are:
(a) **ou** = **ow**, as in **bough** (b) **ou** = long **oo** sound, as in **troupe**
(c) **ou** = short **u** sound, as in **rough**.
Look closely at the words in the box. Say them quietly to yourself. Write each under its correct heading below.

youth	hound	group	touch
flounder	soup	devour	you
double	cousin	trouble	astound

ou = ow sound	ou = long oo sound	ou = short u sound
______	______	______
______	______	______
______	______	______
______	______	______

B The letters **ur** sometimes make an **er** sound, as in **fur** and **hurt**. Write each **ur** word from the box beside its meaning below.

hamburger	furniture	turkey	absurd	suburb	sunburn
murder	turnip	surgeon	purchase	urgent	burden

1. stupid, ridiculous ______________
2. root vegetable ______________
3. tables, chairs ______________
4. takeaway food ______________
5. type of doctor ______________
6. buy ______________
7. needing immediate attention ______________
8. load ______________
9. outskirts of a city ______________
10. farmyard bird ______________
11. kill illegally ______________
12. skin damage from the sun ______________

Parent/Teacher Signature   Date

Revision

A Add au, aw or ea to complete each word.

1. squ____k (noise of a mouse)
2. c____liflower (vegetable)
3. scr____l (untidy writing)
4. t____cher (tutor)
5. fl____ (fault)
6. s____sage (mince meat in casing)
7. s____son (time of the year)
8. cl____ (a crab has one)
9. t____t (tight)
10. outl____ (bushranger)
11. ____ction (sale)
12. dr____d (fear)

B Add or, ow or ou to complete the words.

1. sparr____ (small bird)
2. m____sel (small scrap of food)
3. fl____nder (fish)
4. s____p (liquid food)
5. elb____ (joint of the arm)
6. abs____b (soak up)
7. n____th (direction)
8. shall____ (not deep)
9. h____nd (dog)
10. t____ch (feel)
11. burr____ (home of a rabbit)
12. ac____n (seed of the oak tree)

C Add a sound unit to complete the words.

1. t____key (farmyard bird)
2. c____sin (relation)
3. st____ple (part of a church)
4. c____ard (person not brave)
5. h____x (trick, ruse)
6. h____net (large wasp)
7. dr____sy (sleepy)
8. s____geon (doctor who operates)
9. l____the (hate, detest)
10. p____der (fine dust)
11. m____sture (trace of liquid)
12. bamb____ (tall grass)

Parent/Teacher Signature Date

UNIT 26

Test 1

The underlined words are spelled incorrectly. Write the words correctly on the line.

1	We sold our house by orction.	1
2	I ate the delicious strorberries.	2
3	This farmer grew collieflowers on his land.	3
4	Our new teecher comes from Darwin.	4
5	Last night she dremed about dinosaurs.	5
6	The wether is quite rainy today.	6
7	I hope you suckceed with your work.	7
8	The referey blew the whistle to end the match.	8
9	The lowves of bread are on the table.	9
10	The pollen in the air made her sneize.	10
11	He has a lot of swet on his forehead.	11
12	I enjoy eating cereal for brakefast.	12

Total correct ______ / 12

Parent/Teacher Signature Date

Test 2

Choose the correct spelling from the words in the brackets. Write the word on the line.

1	A (surgon, surgeon, sergeon) sewed his wound.	1
2	The car's gears are (automatic, ortomatic, ortimatic).	2
3	Billy is very tall and (orkward, awkwood, awkward).	3
4	We are having roast (terky, turky, turkey) for dinner.	4
5	I had tomato (supe, soop, soup) for tea.	5
6	They have expensive (furniture, ferniture, furnitchure).	6
7	The (vowels, vowals, vallows) are a, e, i, o and u.	7
8	The new bridge is (enormus, enormous, enormas).	8
9	I felt really (drowsy, drousy, drozee) after the run.	9
10	A (cockatu, cokatu, cockatoo) lives in the hollow log.	10
11	These toadstools are (poisonus, poisunas, poisonous).	11
12	The (referee, rafari, refaree) sent the player off.	12

Total correct ______ / 12

Parent/Teacher Signature

Date

UNIT 28

Adding the suffix ion 1

A When you add **ion** to the endings of some words you do not have to make any changes to the spelling of the word.
Example: act + ion = action
Make the word in brackets at the end of each sentence end in **ion**. Write the word in the space.

1. Her quick ________________ surprised us all. (act)
2. She showed a great deal of ________________ towards the puppy. (affect)
3. We had to do a lot of ________________ sums. (subtract)
4. The weather bureau made an odd ________________. (predict)
5. The chemicals led to the ________________ of certain species of fish. (extinct)
6. The boy made a deep ________________ on the teachers. (impress)
7. The university graduate is not sure what ________________ to follow. (profess)
8. The new student made a funny ________________. (express)
9. We had to make a quick ________________ of what we wanted. (select)
10. The soldier acted with ________________ during the battle. (distinct)

B For some words you must drop letters to add **ion**.
Examples: generate, generation; induce, induction
Make each word in the brackets end in **ion**. Write it in the space. (Some of the words will be in plural form.)

1. I offered my ________________ to the bride and groom. (congratulate)
2. This is a really good ________________ of the real thing. (imitate)
3. I hope we do not get any ________________ with the process. (complicate)
4. We placed all the ________________ around the hall. (decorate)
5. He hopes to get a good ________________ at the college. (educate)
6. The ________________ of the two schools caused lots of problems. (separate)
7. The ________________ of cars at this factory has increased. (produce)
8. At the ball the host made all the ________________. (introduce)
9. The ________________ of a new college helped us all. (create)
10. There will be a great ________________ in donations this year. (reduce)

Parent/Teacher Signature Date

Adding the suffix ion 2

For some words you have to change the final letter or letters before adding the suffix **ion**. Study these examples carefully and then complete the activities.

Change **t** to **ss** and add **ion**. Example: remit, remission
Change **de** to **s** and add **ion**. Example: intrude, intrusion
Change **e** to **at** or **it** and add **ion**.
Examples: machine, machination; expose, exposition

A Make the word in brackets end in ion. Write it in the space.

1. We asked ____________________ to go down the street. (permit)
2. The ____________________ ruined the land. (erode)
3. A fatal ____________________ occurred at the crossroads. (collide)
4. A loud ____________________ could be heard all over the city. (explode)
5. The first television ____________________ took place in the 1950s. (transmit)
6. At the ____________________ of the ceremony we left. (conclude)
7. She has been an ____________________ to all of us. (inspire)
8. There was a lot of ____________________ to the new law. (oppose)
9. The doctor made a thorough ____________________ of the patient. (examine)
10. The dictionary gave a clear ____________________ of the word. (define)

B Make these words end in ion and write them in sentences.

1. discuss ____
2. contract ____
3. generate ____
4. imitate ____
5. complicate ____
6. persuade ____
7. explore ____
8. combine ____

Parent/Teacher Signature Date

Adding the suffixes able and ible

A For many words you can add the suffixes **able** and **ible** without changing the spelling of a word, such as **readable**, or they are simply added to a root word, such as **legible**, from the root word **lego** (read).
Use a word from the box to complete each sentence.

profitable	remarkable	laughable	edible	possible	visible
perishable	dependable	expendable	terrible	legible	audible

1. Keep this food cold as it is quite ________________.
2. Cooper is a very ________________ student.
3. The fete we conducted was very ________________.
4. It was a ________________ achievement.
5. Don't worry if you lose some because these are quite ________________.
6. His sudden change in attitude was really quite ________________.
7. The plane is now ________________ through the clouds.
8. The voice of the comedian was ________________ in the large hall.
9. This kind of fungus is not poisonous and is quite ________________.
10. His writing is now ________________ after all the practice he has put in.
11. I don't think it will be ________________ for him to win the race.
12. A ________________ accident occurred here last night.

B For words that end in **e** you drop the **e** when adding **able**. However, if a word ends in a soft **ce** or **ge** you retain the **e**.
Examples: live, livable; trace, traceable
Make these words end in **able**.

1. change ____________	5. peace ____________	9. presume ____________
2. desire ____________	6. service ____________	10. compare ____________
3. love ____________	7. notice ____________	11. manage ____________
4. deplore ____________	8. use ____________	12. excuse ____________

Parent/Teacher Signature Date

UNIT 31

Adding the suffix ed

When you add **ed** to some words no changes are needed. Example: heap, heaped. If a word ends in **e**, drop the **e** and then add **ed**. Example: believe, believed
If a word ends in a vowel followed by a consonant, double the final letter. Example: chop, chopped
If a word ends in **y**, change the **y** to **i** before adding **ed**. Example: rely, relied

A Complete each sentence by adding **ed** to each word in the box and writing it in the space below.

describe	**knit**	**deny**	**bury**	**travel**	**drip**
brush	**waste**	**reply**	**stop**	**stir**	**hurry**

1. Emily ____________ her hair before going to school.
2. The boys ____________ a lot of time being silly.
3. The witness ____________ the thief to the police.
4. The thief ____________ snatching the bag of jewels.
5. The tap ____________ most of the night.
6. The children ____________ because they knew they were late.
7. She ____________ to his question as best she could.
8. The dog ____________ the bone in the backyard.
9. Thomas ____________ to America on a large jet liner.
10. Sophie ____________ the contents of the pot with a large fork.
11. Ethan ____________ his little sister a pair of woollen gloves.
12. The bus ____________ at the corner.

B Make these words end in **ed**.

1. study ____________	5. celebrate ____________	9. shop ____________
2. capture ____________	6. continue ____________	10. relax ____________
3. copy ____________	7. chop ____________	11. chase ____________
4. explore ____________	8. prefer ____________	12. qualify ____________

Parent/Teacher Signature Date

UNIT 32

Revision

A Make each word end in **able** and write the word in a sentence of your own.

1. agree ______________________________
2. afford ______________________________
3. punish ______________________________
4. profit ______________________________
5. expand ______________________________

B Add **able** or **ible** to complete each word.

1. a comfort______ chair
2. leg______ writing
3. combust______ material
4. a cred______ story
5. a remark______ story
6. a predict______ event
7. a reli______ student
8. a navig______ river
9. a valu______ pearl
10. a respect______ score
11. a refill______ container
12. a horr______ accident

C Make the word in brackets end in **ed**. Make spelling changes if they are needed.

1. ________________ accurately (describe)
2. ________________ hard (study)
3. ________________ quickly (chop)
4. ________________ obstinately (continue)
5. ________________ deeply (bury)
6. ________________ far (travel)
7. ________________ carefully (brush)
8. ________________ lovingly (hug)
9. ________________ sharply (reply)
10. ________________ quickly (stir)
11. ________________ constantly (drip)
12. ________________ happily (celebrate)

Parent/Teacher Signature Date

Test

The underlined word in each sentence is spelled incorrectly. Write it correctly on the line.

	Sentence	
1	These crimes are punishible by prison sentences.	1
2	It was really a horable accident.	2
3	This material is combustable in the heat.	3
4	The dog buryed the bone on the lawn.	4
5	We have traveled a long way.	5
6	I asked for purmission to go down the street.	6
7	At the conclushon of the match I went home.	7
8	The new student made a good impreshun on everyone.	8
9	Jack is getting a good edukation at his school.	9
10	The deckoration on the cake looked delightful.	10
11	She showered a lot of afecction on the puppy.	11
12	A loud exploshun could be heard from far away.	12

Total correct ______ / 12

Parent/Teacher Signature   Date

UNIT 34

Compound words

Compound words are two or more words joined together to make a new word. Examples:
black + bird = blackbird; rain + bow = rainbow

A Write the correct word from the box at the end of each word below to make a compound word.

quake	**line**	**where**	**roads**	**glasses**	**stack**
light	**writer**	**print**	**out**	**back**	**stairs**

1. hay__________
2. cross__________
3. earth__________
4. else__________
5. pipe__________
6. sun__________
7. down__________
8. horse__________
9. look__________
10. finger__________
11. sign__________
12. star__________

B Add a compound word from the box to each sentence.

headphones	**lifejackets**	**backyard**	**campfire**	**seagull**	**roadworks**
lifesavers	**fireproof**	**landmark**	**barefoot**	**landfill**	**overboard**

1. My brothers and I play cricket in our ____________________.
2. At the beach was a ____________________ with only one leg.
3. We were all told to put on our ____________________ when the sea became rough.
4. She listened to the music through her ____________________.
5. The ____________________ that was left burning caused the bushfire.
6. The ____________________ raced to help the drowning surfers.
7. There is a detour because of the ____________________.
8. The drunken sailor fell ____________________.
9. The rubbish was taken to the ____________________.
10. As his parents were so poor he went to school ____________________.
11. This old homestead is a real ____________________ in our region.
12. This ____________________ suit is used by firefighters.

Parent/Teacher Signature Date

Internal double consonants

Double consonants occur naturally in some words, while others occur because a prefix or suffix is added. Examples: carrot, irreversible

A Write each word in the box beside its meaning below.

daffodil	**rabbit**	**jewellery**	**alligator**	**mammoth**	**mannequin**
moccasin	**accelerate**	**corridor**	**gorilla**	**mayonnaise**	**hurricane**

1. large ape ________________
2. to go faster ________________
3. small furry animal ________________
4. large reptile ________________
5. model ________________
6. destructive wind ________________
7. passage, hallway ________________
8. extinct elephant-like animal ____________
9. flower ________________
10. soft footwear ________________
11. necklaces and bangles ______________
12. salad dressing ________________

B Choose a set of double letters from the box to write in the spaces below. Use each set of double letters twice.

nn	pp	ss	rr	tt	zz

1. bu____ard (large bird
2. aba____oir (meat works
3. mu____on (meat of a sheep)
4. profe____or (learned teacher)
5. hi____opotamus (large animal)
6. bli____ard (snowstorm)
7. squi____el (small anmal)
8. pa____enger (person being driven)
9. sa____hire (a precious blue stone)
10. i____ocent (not guilty)
11. po____idge (oatmeal)
12. ante____a (aerial for a television)

C Choose the correct set of double letters to fill the spaces.

1. pu____in (bird)
   ff, mm
2. che____ar (cheese)
   tt, dd
3. bro____oli (vegetable)
   bb, cc
4. sa____le (riding seat)
   dd, pp
5. exa____erate (overstate)
   mm, gg
6. a____ic (top room)
   zz, tt

Parent/Teacher Signature   Date

Portmanteau words

A portmanteau word is one that has been made up by blending two other words together. They were first used by the author Lewis Carrol who wrote *Alice in Wonderland.* For example, he made the word **chortle** from **chuckle** and **snort**.

A Write the two words from which each of these words have come.

1. flare = ____________ + ____________
2. brunch = ____________ + ____________
3. moped = ____________ + ____________
4. motel = ____________ + ____________
5. smog = ____________ + ____________
6. medicare = ____________ + ____________
7. breathalyser = ____________ + ____________
8. heliport = ____________ + ____________
9. newscast = ____________ + ____________
10. telecast = ____________ + ____________

B Write the word we use that has been developed from these words.

1. parachute + troopers = ________________
2. glare + shimmer = ________________
3. twist + swirl = ________________
4. motor + parade = ________________
5. melody + drama = ________________
6. not + ever = ________________
7. squirm + wriggle = ________________
8. high + fidelity = ________________
9. automatic + bank = ________________
10. smack + bash = ________________

C Make up your own portmanteau words. For example, **pen** + **book** could be **penook**.
Write two words to form your two portmanteau words.

1. ________________ + ________________ = ______________________________
2. ________________ + ________________ = ______________________________

Parent/Teacher Signature Date

Sound patterns, er

Many words contain the **er** sound, as in **feather** and **desert**.

A Write each word in the correct space.

certain	1. The ______________ was placed on the table between the dishes.
battery	2. This factory has a lot of high-tech ______________.
camera	3. After running a distance Joshua began to ______________ freely.
liberty	4. The seedlings were raised in the plant ______________.
perspire	5. I am ______________ that Charlotte will excel in the test.
nursery	6. She took lots of photographs with her ______________.
machinery	7. Our teacher has very ______________ ideas about education.
cutlery	8. Lily ______________ to her friend so the teacher would not hear.
modern	9. The prisoners long for their ______________.
whispered	10. When the lights were left on the car ______________ became flat.

B Each **er** word in the box can be linked in some way to a word below. Write each word in the space.

litter	**miserable**	**interfere**	**revolver**	**saucer**	**rhinoceros**
answered	**verse**	**laughter**	**fever**	**passenger**	**stationery**

1. illness ______________
2. unhappy ______________
3. cup ______________
4. rubbish ______________
5. replied ______________
6. happiness ______________
7. train ______________
8. envelopes ______________
9. bullets ______________
10. meddle ______________
11. poem ______________
12. animal ______________

C Write these **er** words in sentences of your own:

deserve ______________________________

several ______________________________

Parent/Teacher Signature Date

Sound patterns, a

A The letter **a** often has an **ar** sound as in **mask** and **bath**. Find the words in the grid and write them next to the correct meaning.

k	o	a	l	a	b
p	c	a	l	f	a
a	m	a	s	t	n
l	c	a	l	m	a
m	f	a	s	t	n
g	l	a	s	s	a
b	a	s	k	e	t
f	l	a	s	k	x

1. container for liquid ______
2. not nervous ______
3. very quick ______
4. part of your hand ______
5. part of a sailing ship ______
6. yellow fruit ______
7. clear window material ______
8. newborn cow ______
9. Australian marsupial ______
10. object for carrying things in ______

B Sometimes the letter **a** has a short **o** sound, as in **wash** and **wallow**.
The first syllable of each word in the box contains an **a** as a short **o** sound. Write each beside its correct meaning below.

swan	**wallet**	**squash**	**quarrel**	**wallaby**	**watched**
waratah	**swamp**	**squadron**	**quantity**	**washer**	**quarry**

1. Australian flower ______
2. group of war planes ______
3. cleaner ______
4. where stone is mined ______
5. observed ______
6. vegetable or game ______
7. money holder ______
8. hopping marsupial ______
9. amount ______
10. argument ______
11. wet bushland area ______
12. graceful waterbird ______

C Write these words in sentences of your own:

nasty ______

quality ______

Parent/Teacher Signature ______ Date ______

Complex consonant groups, ch and tch

A The letters **ch** can represent three sounds: (a) **ch** sound as in **chop** (b) **k** sound as in **chemist** (c) **sh** sound as in **chef**. Write each word from the box in its correct sentence.

charity
quench
cherry
chaff
chaplain
chapel
chemical
chemist
chaos
machine
champagne
parachute

1. We got the medicine from the ______________ shop.
2. The couple had their wedding in the small ______________.
3. The ______________ at our school often counsels students.
4. I decided to ______________ my thirst as it was so hot.
5. He donated all the money to a deserving ______________.
6. Don't ingest that ______________ as it is toxic.
7. There was a great deal of ______________ when the train crashed.
8. To celebrate her win she drank some ______________.
9. This ______________ stamps out shapes from flat steel sheets.
10. The paratrooper landed safely by using a ______________.
11. We fed the horse some ______________ and oats.
12. The ______________ I ate was juicy and delicious.

B The letter pattern **tch** comes after a short vowel. However, five common words sound **tch** but end in **ch**. These are **such**, **rich**, **much**, **which** and **sandwich**.
Write each **tch** word from the box beside its meaning.

satchel	**catch**	**bitch**	**stretch**	**itch**	**britches**
witch	**latch**	**batch**	**match**	**kitchen**	**watch**

1. timepiece ______________
2. part of a door lock ______________
3. female dog ______________
4. fairytale character ______________
5. carrying case for papers ______________
6. to grab hold of ______________
7. to reach out ______________
8. clothing ______________
9. stick that lights fires ______________
10. skin annoyance ______________
11. group of items ______________
12. cooking room ______________

Parent/Teacher Signature　　　　　　　　　　Date

UNIT 40

Sound patterns, y

A The letter **y** is often pronounced as a long **i** sound, as in **my** and **reply**.
Write each word from the box beside its meaning below.

multiply	**hyphen**	**hydrant**	**hygienic**	**flyer**	**clarify**
nylon	**cyclone**	**python**	**rhyming**	**magnify**	**dyeing**

1. large snake ________________
2. destructive wind ________________
3. artificial material ________________
4. punctuation mark ________________
5. water outlet ________________
6. healthy, clean living ________________
7. person who flies ________________
8. colouring ________________
9. to make clear ________________
10. sounding the same ________________
11. to make larger ________________
12. to increase ________________

B Sometimes the letter **y** at the end of a word is a long **e** sound, as in **plenty** and **lily**. The letter **y** in the middle of a word is sometimes a short **i** sound, as in **physics**.
Write each word from the box in its correct sentence.

pansy
mystery
platypus
safety
empty
poultry
guilty
luckily
easily
laundry
any
rapidly

1. This bottle is full but that one is ________________.
2. On the ________________ farm there were lots of hens and chicks.
3. The jury found the person ________________ of theft.
4. The kangaroo quite ________________ jumped the fence.
5. We washed and dried the clothes in the ________________.
6. It was a complete ________________ as to where it had gone.
7. There was a bad accident but ________________ no one was hurt.
8. The boy rode ________________ to the town to break the news.
9. It is a job that ________________ person could do as it is so easy.
10. I picked the ________________ and put it in a vase on the table.
11. The ________________ is really an odd creature.
12. When the storm raged we ran for the ________________ of the room.

Parent/Teacher Signature   Date

Complex consonant groups, dge and ck

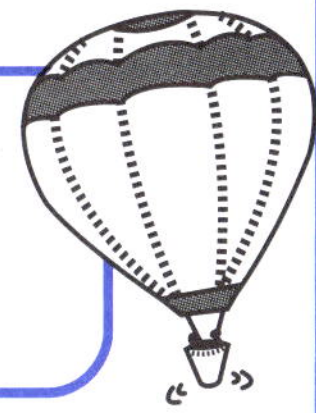

A The letter pattern **dge** only follows a short vowel, as in **edge** and **budge**.
Write each word from the box in its correct sentence.

badge
edge
ledge
judge
porridge
gadget
fudge
knowledge
hedge
dodge

1. The children peered over the ______________ of the steep cliff.
2. You should spend plenty of time acquiring ________________.
3. For dessert he had a bowl of chocolate ______________.
4. For breakfast I had a bowl of ______________.
5. William wore his club's ______________ on his lapel.
6. The home was surrounded by a neatly cut ______________.
7. He grabbed the ball and then tried to ___________ his opponent.
8. We put the vases on the ______________ of the kitchen cupboard.
9. The ______________ sentenced the criminal to jail.
10. This little ______________ is quite useful around the house.

B The letter pattern **ck** is called two-letter **k**. It is only used after a short vowel, as in **duck** and **pack**.
Write each **ck** word from the box beside its meaning below.

wicked	**jacket**	**wicket**	**buckle**	**locker**	**hockey**
chuckle	**stocking**	**locket**	**paddock**	**quickly**	**cockatoo**

1. giggle ____________________
2. rapidly ___________________
3. leg covering ____________________
4. light coat ____________________
5. evil ____________________
6. part of a belt ____________________
7. sport ____________________
8. Australian parrot ____________________
9. field ____________________
10. small storage box ____________________
11. used in a cricket game ____________
12. piece of jewellery _______________

Parent/Teacher Signature Date

UNIT 42

Complex consonant groups, th and sh

A The letter pattern **th** has two sounds:
(a) unvoiced, as in **thin** (b) voiced, as in **then**.
Write each word from the box in its correct sentence (only one has a voiced **th**).

author
thumb
leather
thistles
eighth
faithful
marathon
feather
warmth
thermal
theology
therefore

1. The dog remained loyal and ______________ to its master.
2. The sharp ______________ scratched my legs.
3. She hopes to become a priest so she will study ______________.
4. This is the ______________ day of the month.
5. The ______________ has written a sequel to her first book.
6. The ______________ pool was boiling hot.
7. He missed the nail with the hammer and hit his ____________.
8. Mia is quite ill and ______________ will not be here this afternoon.
9. The shoes were made of the ______________ from crocodile skins.
10. Thomas won the ______________ at the last Olympic Games.
11. The ______________ from the fire melted the ice.
12. The sparrow placed the ______________ in its nest to make it soft.

B The letters **sh** are usually pronounced as in **fish** or **shelf**.
Write each **sh** word from the box beside its meaning below.

demolish	**bishop**	**marsh**	**vanish**	**mushroom**
accomplish	**extinguish**	**perish**	**astonish**	**shriek**

1. achieve ____________________
2. douse a flame ____________________
3. die or pass away ____________________
4. wet boggy area ________________
5. knock down a building ______________
6. amaze ____________________
7. squeal loudly ____________________
8. kind of fungus ____________________
9. disappear ____________________
10. senior church official _______________

Parent/Teacher Signature Date

Revision

A Sort the words in the box under their headings below.

flyer	physical	guilty	nylon	python	pansy
mysterious	empty	cyclone	platypus	hyphen	hygiene

y = long i sound | **y = long e sound** | **y = short i sound**

______ ______ ______ ______

______ ______ ______ ______

______ ______ ______ ______

B Add th, sh or ck in the spaces.

1. vani____ (disappear)
2. ja____et (light coat)
3. au____or (book writer)
4. wi____ed (evil)
5. mu____room (fungus)
6. mara____on (long foot race)
7. warm____ (heat)
8. fini____ed (ended)
9. fai____ful (loyal)
10. ho____ey (sport)
11. cu____ion (pillow)
12. bu____le (part of a belt)

C Sort the words in the box under their headings below.

swan	fast	quarrel	wallaby	quarry	flask
palm	wattle	calf	basket	glass	watch

a = ar sound | **a = short o sound**

______ ______ ______ ______

______ ______ ______ ______

______ ______ ______ ______

Parent/Teacher Signature Date

Test 1

The underlined words are spelled incorrectly. Write the correct spelling on the line.

1. There is a lot of <u>machinary</u> on this farm. 1
2. The angry <u>rhinocaros</u> charged the tourists. 2
3. The poem has six <u>vurses</u>. 3
4. The <u>koarla</u> is an Australian native animal. 4
5. Oliver lost his <u>wollat</u> with fifty dollars in it. 5
6. The boys had a long <u>quarral</u> about the marbles. 6
7. He was wearing a <u>parashute</u> when he jumped out. 7
8. We cooked the meals in the <u>kichen</u>. 8
9. This <u>mashine</u> can make small cars. 9
10. I like to <u>quentch</u> my thirst with cold water. 10
11. The ocean was quite <u>carlm</u> today. 11
12. We got the gravel from a nearby <u>qorry</u>. 12

Total correct ______ / 12

Parent/Teacher Signature Date

Test 2

Choose the correct spelling of each word in the brackets and write it on the line.

1 Jack has a lot of (knoledge, knowledge, noledge). ______ 1

2 The ball knocked the (wickets, wikits, whickets) over. ______ 2

3 We tried to (extingwish, extingish, extinguish) the fire. ______ 3

4 We ate the tasty (mushroom, machroom, mushroome). ______ 4

5 The dog is very (fathful, faithfull, faithful). ______ 5

6 We are (dying, dyeing, diing) the clothes a red colour. ______ 6

7 The (syclone, ciclone, cyclone) caused great damage. ______ 7

8 I made a (hyfen, hyphen, hyphan) in my book. ______ 8

9 We won the race (eesily, easily, easaly). ______ 9

10 The boys rushed to the (safety, safty, saftey) of the room. ______ 10

11 The fishing line is made of (nilon, nighlon, nylon). ______ 11

12 She wore a (loket, lockat, locket) around her neck. ______ 12

Total correct ______ / 12

Parent/Teacher Signature   Date

UNIT 46

Adding ing, words ending in a consonant

If a word ends in two consonants no spelling changes are required when you add **ing**.
Example: bang, banging

When you add **ing** to words ending in a short vowel followed by a consonant you must double the consonant. Examples: hop, hopping; flap, flapping

A Make the words in brackets at the end of each sentence below end in **ing**. Write the word on the line.

1. Our team is easily ______________ the match. (win)
2. My trousers seem to keep ______________ each day. (shrink)
3. Sophie and I are ______________ to school. (walk)
4. The boys, who got up late, are now ______________ for the bus. (rush)
5. The dogs are ______________ the rabbits. (catch)
6. I am ______________ a new bike for a birthday present. (get)
7. Mike is ______________ some wood for the fire. (chop)
8. We are going ______________ after school. (shop)
9. The children are ______________ the trees along the creek. (plant)
10. We went ______________ for gold last week. (pan)
11. The dog is ______________ for a scrap of food. (beg)
12. Emily is ______________ the punctured tyre. (mend)
13. Tom is ______________ quickly around the school yard. (skip)
14. The workers are ______________ the seedlings in the pots. (thin)
15. Chloe is ______________ across the pool. (swim)
16. The birds are ______________ their wings quickly. (flap)

B Make these words end in **ing** and then write them in sentences of your own:

1. tear ______________________________
2. wrap ______________________________

Parent/Teacher Signature Date

Adding ing, words ending in e or y

If a word ends in a silent **e** you drop the **e** when adding **ing**. Examples: hate, hating; come, coming

Note: Do not drop the **e** if there is a vowel before the final **e**. Example: see, seeing

If a word ends in **y** you simply add **ing**.
Example: try, trying

A Make the word in brackets at the end of each sentence below end in **ing**. Write the word on the line.

1. The boys are ______________ to the disco. (come)
2. Some vandals are ______________ the walls. (damage)
3. The dog is ______________ the cat. (chase)
4. The adults are ______________ the fighting children. (separate)
5. The people are ______________ in the line. (queue)
6. I am ______________ a new car from this dealership. (purchase)
7. The campers are ______________ along the stream. (canoe)
8. I am ______________ where the last tourists went. (see)
9. The bully is ______________ the small boys to give him some money. (force)
10. The dog is ______________ the stranger on the leg. (bite)
11. I am ______________ I win first prize. (hope)
12. The girls are ______________ the lollies with their classmates. (share)
13. The shooter was ______________ at the birds. (fire)
14. The girls are ______________ into the cool water. (dive)
15. Josh is ______________ his new leather shoes. (shine)
16. Jack is ______________ the latest gadget on his mobile phone. (use)

B Make these words end in **ing** and then write them in sentences of your own:

1. take ______________________________
2. weave ______________________________

Parent/Teacher Signature   Date

UNIT 48

Prefixes 1

Prefixes are groups of letters added to the beginning of words. The only rule to remember when adding a prefix is to do just that — add it. You do not have to make spelling changes.
Examples: in + visible = invisible; un + well = unwell

A The words in the box each contain a prefix. Use the words to complete the sentences below.

inland	**antidote**	**midday**	**telescope**	**remount**
emigrate	**outlaw**	**unpopular**	**transplant**	**postpone**

1. The explorers struggled further ________________.
2. We ate our lunch about ________________.
3. Because of the rain we decided to ________________ the cricket match.
4. As he is so selfish Lachlan is the most ________________ boy in the class.
5. After she was bitten by the spider Mia was given an ________________.
6. The refugees decided to ________________ to another country.
7. The sheriff cornered the ________________ in the saloon.
8. The ship's captain studied the faraway land through a ________________.
9. When she fell off, the jockey decided to quickly ________________ the horse.
10. We decided to ________________ the seedlings from the box into the garden.

B Make a new word by adding the correct prefix in the box to the words below.

dis	un	im	il

1. ____possible	5. ____legible	9. ____tie
2. ____necessary	6. ____appoint	10. ____literate
3. ____appear	7. ____sure	11. ____count
4. ____legal	8. ____polite	12. ____patient

Parent/Teacher Signature Date

Prefixes 2

Prefixes are letters added to the beginning of a word. No spelling changes are needed.
Examples: in + visible = invisible; un + well = unwell

A Add the correct prefix from the box to complete the words below.

pre	tri	re	in	ex	uni	un	non	dis	mis

1. Only a silly student likes to _____behave at school.
2. These new shoes were really quite _____expensive.
3. Our school has a blue-coloured _____form.
4. What he said was really a lot of _____sense.
5. I am _____certain whether I will be allowed to come.
6. She caught the _____press train to the city this morning.
7. We watched as the jet _____appeared above the clouds.
8. You must always take some _____cautions before using chemicals.
9. Mike is going to take part in the _____athlon next Saturday.
10. The police hope to soon _____capture the escaped convict.

B Add prefixes to these words to make them mean the opposite. Example: un + well = unwell

1. _____dress	**3. _____allow**	**5. _____complete**	**7. _____armed**
2. _____like	**4. _____equal**	**6. _____popular**	**8. _____lead**

C Complete the sentences by adding words to these prefixes.

1. A rumour that is false is un___________.
2. A rude person is im___________.
3. Something out of sight is in___________.
4. People who dis___________ hold different points of view.
5. An un___________ person is sad.
6. Something that does not make sense is really non___________.
7. A person who steals is dis___________.

Parent/Teacher Signature Date

UNIT 50

Revision

A Add the suffix **ing** to the words in the box and write them under the correct heading below.

get	**walk**	**dive**	**rush**
shrink	**purchase**	**skip**	**chase**
separate	**shop**	**catch**	**pan**

No change	**Double last letter**	**Drop e**
________________	________________	________________
________________	________________	________________
________________	________________	________________
________________	________________	________________

B Add a suitable prefix to complete each word.

1. I think I really _____judged Sophie as she is really nice after all.
2. It is important to _____heat this food before serving it.
3. The teacher asked me to _____write my story neatly.
4. I couldn't wait to _____wrap my present.
5. He completely _____regarded the advice he was given.
6. Mr Smith's _____come is $50,000 a year.
7. The teacher told us we could not leave as our stories were _____complete.
8. This restaurant is a _____smoking one.
9. My little sister attends _____school.
10. The atomic _____marine dived beneath the surface of the ocean.

Parent/Teacher Signature   Date

Test

Choose the correct prefix from the options in brackets to complete the words.

1 The boy was suspended from school for _____conduct. (en, ex, mis)

2 We were lucky the bomb did not _____plode. (in, ex, bi)

3 These books are not available _____versally. (ex, uni, tri)

4 The coach really tries to _____courage us. (fore, in, en)

5 The _____caster said it would soon rain again. (en, uni, fore)

6 He tried hard not to _____spell any words. (mis, pre, dis)

7 We learned about dinosaurs in _____historic times. (pre, mis, ex)

8 The new student _____obeyed the orders of the principal. (mis, non, dis)

9 He was really quite _____contented with his friends' attitude. (mis, dis, ex)

10 This charity is a _____profit organisation. (im, in, non)

11 He received a blow to his _____head. (en, fore, non)

12 Be careful you do not _____danger other students. (en, ex, mis)

Total correct _____
12

Parent/Teacher Signature   Date

UNIT 52

Contractions

Sometimes we combine two words and shorten them by leaving out a letter or letters. We put an apostrophe to show where the letters are missing. Examples: are + not = aren't; they + are = they're

A Write the two words that make up each underlined contraction.

1. You're very tall. __________ __________
2. I've not had my tea yet. __________ __________
3. You'd better hurry up. __________ __________
4. You mustn't be late again. __________ __________
5. I didn't see who did it. __________ __________
6. Flies don't bother me. __________ __________
7. Riley wasn't in the room when it happened. __________ __________
8. I couldn't eat all my lunch. __________ __________
9. We hadn't gone far when the car had a puncture. __________ __________
10. The dog wouldn't leave its kennel. __________ __________

B Choose the correct contraction in the brackets to complete the sentences.

1. I definitely ______________ help you again. (weren't, won't)
2. Jack ______________ be so rude. (shouldn't, who'd)
3. We did not know ______________ left. (where'd, they'd)
4. ______________ late again. (Your, You're)
5. ______________ quite warm today. (It's, Its)
6. The girls ______________ arrived yet. (hasn't, haven't)
7. I ______________ have your missing football. (doesn't, don't)
8. I'm sure ______________ find out the answer soon. (you'll, you've)
9. The girls ______________ brought their equipment. (hasn't, haven't)
10. They ______________ in the room at the time. (wasn't, weren't)

Parent/Teacher Signature Date

Words we often confuse

Sometimes we make errors in spelling because we use an incorrect but similar word when writing.

Choose the correct word in the brackets to complete each sentence.

1. Michelle suddenly fell ________ the bridge. (of, off)
2. I will certainly ________ your kind invitation. (accept, except)
3. ________ going to help us pick up the rubbish. (There, They're)
4. Ethan wrote a ________ to cover the cost of the repairs. (check, cheque)
5. It didn't take long for the student to ________ to the rules. (adapt, adopt)
6. Her writing is so careless it is ________. (illegible, eligible)
7. Peter said it was ________ warm in Adelaide yesterday. (quite, quiet)
8. The feathery seeds were ________ away by the wind. (born, borne)
9. I ordered apple strudel for my ________. (desert, dessert)
10. The professor is an ________ scientist. (imminent, eminent)
11. This part of the motor was found to be ________. (deficient, defective)
12. Three other people ________ Alice had the opportunity to steal the money. (beside, besides)
13. We made a makeshift tent from the sheet of ________. (canvas, canvass)
14. He ________ a new bicycle as a birthday present. (chose, choose)
15. Cancer is a nasty ________ to have. (decease, disease)
16. I ________ the shovel against the wall. (leant, lent)

Parent/Teacher Signature Date

UNIT 54

Where animal names come from

Many animal names come from words in languages other than English.

Match the creatures listed in the box with the words described below.

orangutan	**duck**	**leopard**	**poodle**	**raccoon**	**spider**
crocodile	**flamingo**	**caterpillar**	**porcupine**	**octopus**	**dinosaur**

1. From the Old English word spithra, meaning spinner.

   ____

2. From the North American Indian word raugraughcan, meaning scratcher.

   ____

3. From the German word pudelhund, meaning splash dog.

   ____

4. From the French words porc d'espine, meaning spine porker.

   ____

5. From the Greek words octo and pous, meaning eight foot.

   ____

6. From the Malay word oranghutan, meaning forest man.

   ____

7. From the Greek word krokodellos, meaning gravel-worm.

   ____

8. From the Latin word deinos-sauros, meaning fearful lizard.

   ____

9. From the Old English word duce, meaning diver.

   ____

10. From the Latin word flamma, meaning flame.

    ____

11. From the Greek word leopardos, meaning lion-tiger.

    ____

12. From the Latin words catta and pilosus, meaning hairy cat.

    ____

Did you know?

The word **animal** comes from the Latin word **anima**, meaning **breath of life**. Animators give the breath of life to pictures.

Parent/Teacher Signature Date

Silent letters

Many words contain silent, or unsounded, letters. In the past some of these letters were sounded and have been left in the word even though today they are silent, as in **calf** and **knee**.

An American, Noah Webster, spent his life making a study of the English language and wanted silent letters to be dropped to make words easier to spell. Unfortunately for students, he did not get his way.

A Write these words adding the missing silent letter.

1. lam__ (baby sheep)
2. de__t (money owed)
3. this__le (prickly plant)
4. cas__le (large home for royalty)
5. dou__t (uncertainty)
6. __nock (hit)
7. thum__ (digit of the hand)
8. We__nesday (day of the week)
9. hym__ (sacred song)
10. of__en (many times)
11. s__issors (cutting implement)
12. __nife (utensil)

B Each of these words contains a silent letter. Match it with its meaning below.

calf knee beret wrong yolk school sword palm

1. not correct ________________
2. place of learning ________________
3. steel weapon ________________
4. part of your hand ________________
5. baby cow ________________
6. soft cap ________________
7. part of an egg ________________
8. joint of the leg ________________

C The incomplete words below each contain a silent letter. Complete the word to match its meaning and circle the silent letter.

1. h_________ (sixty minutes)
2. k______________ (joint of the finger)
3. c_________ (implement for your hair)
4. d______________ (small boat)
5. p___________ (person who mends taps)
6. c____________ (shop to buy medicine)
7. s_____________ (smell)
8. k______________ (found on a door)

Parent/Teacher Signature Date

UNIT 56

Initial consonant blends

Often two consonants are blended to begin the first sound of a word, such as the letters **bl** in **black**.

A Add a pair of letters from the box to complete each word below.

gr	pl	sc	dr	pr	sm
st	cr	fl	cl	fr	sk

1. _____irk (grin)
2. _____arlet (red colour)
3. _____ofessor (learned teacher)
4. _____adual (slowly)
5. _____agile (easily broken)
6. _____atypus (Australian marsupial)
7. _____ayon (drawing rod)
8. _____ought (period without rain)
9. _____ull (the bones of your head)
10. _____orist (flower shop)
11. _____allion (male horse)
12. _____arinet (musical instrument)

B Each word in the box begins with a consonant blend. Write it beside its meaning below.

spaghetti	trombone	twinkle	spinach	snorkel	skeleton
proverb	scald	granite	fragrant	glutton	flamingo

1. to burn with hot water _____________
2. hard rock _____________
3. pleasant smelling _____________
4. musical instrument _____________
5. person who eats too much _____________
6. leafy vegetable _____________
7. bony framework of the body _________
8. large wading bird _____________
9. what stars do _____________
10. kind of pasta _____________
11. wise saying _____________
12. underwater device _________

C Write these words in sentences of your own:

bracelet ____

scavenger ____

procession ____

smudge ____

Parent/Teacher Signature   Date

Hard and soft c

The letter **c** has two main sounds: (a) an **s** sound, called soft **c**, when followed by **e**, **i** or **y**, as in **cell**, **city** and **cycle** (b) a **k** sound, called hard **c**, when followed by **a**, **o**, or **u**, as in **cat**, **cot** and **cut**.

A The words in the box all contain the soft **c** sound. Write each beside a word it can be linked to in some way below.

certain **deceive** **medicine** **cedar** **twice** **cyclone**
celery **justice** **palace** **cigarette** **rhinoceros** **voice**

1. vegetable ________________
2. cheat ________________
3. tree ________________
4. sure ________________
5. tobacco ________________
6. throat ________________
7. double ________________
8. tablet ________________
9. jury ________________
10. king ________________
11. wind ________________
12. elephant ________________

B The words in the box all contain the hard **c** sound. Use each word in its correct sentence below.

cottage **carnival** **correct** **calendar** **compass**
canteen **colony** **country** **canary** **carol**

1. By using the ______________ to find directions they soon arrived safely.
2. The scientist studied the ______________ of ants to discover their habits.
3. We bought lunch at the factory ______________.
4. The family lived in a small ______________ near here.
5. The street ______________ was lots of fun and very colourful.
6. The ______________ in its cage sang many beautiful songs.
7. This one is wrong but the next one is ______________.
8. China is a large and densely populated ______________.
9. We looked up the date of his birthday on the ______________.
10. At Christmas we sang a ______________ about a reindeer.

Parent/Teacher Signature Date

UNIT 58

Hard and soft g

The letter g has two main sounds: (a) a j sound, called soft g, when followed by e, i or y, as in **cage**, **giant** and **gypsy** (b) a g sound, called hard g, when followed by a, o, u or another consonant, as in **game**, **gone**, **gun** and **grand**.

Eight of the words in the box contain the soft g sound and eight contain the hard g sound. Use each to complete the sentences below.

engine	**revenge**	**garlic**	**groan**
genuine	**lounge**	**galaxy**	**guarantee**
giant	**sponge**	**guitar**	**government**
general	**gymnasium**	**guide**	**guard**

1. This machine is small but that one is a ________________.
2. We lazed on the ________________ all day.
3. This is an artificial diamond but that one is ________________
4. The astronomer studied the ________________ through the telescope.
5. The ________________ ordered the soldiers to retreat.
6. The ________________ of this car needs fuel.
7. The pungent odour of the ________________ made me sick.
8. The pain in his stomach made him ________________.
9. The ________________ took the prisoner back to the cell.
10. Jack plays his ________________ when he gets the time.
11. The tour ________________ showed the visitors over the museum.
12. The injured rhinoceros sought ________________ on its tormentors.
13. We work out in the ________________ each day.
14. Charlotte made a ________________ cake to take to the fete.
15. This refrigerator has a ________________ of two years.
16. The ________________ ordered everyone to be inoculated.

Parent/Teacher Signature   Date

Complex consonant groups, ght, nce and nch

A The letters ght are pronounced as a t sound (the g and h are silent) and occur at the end of many words, as in **night** and **bought**. Write each word from the box in its correct sentence.

copyright	brought	delight	midnight	distraught
caught	drought	sought	thought	insight

1. She accepted the award with a great deal of ____________________.
2. Do not photocopy that page as it is ____________________.
3. Joshua ____________________ he saw his old friend at the disco.
4. The tour gave us a good ____________________ into life on a farm.
5. Emily was ____________________ when she could not find her puppy.
6. Oliver ____________________ his brand new bike to school to show his friends.
7. The fish were ____________________ in the net.
8. A long ____________________ has destroyed the cereal crops.
9. The detectives ____________________ only truthful answers from the thieves.
10. He left for home about ____________________.

B The letters nce and nch are also common word endings. Write each word in the box beside a word it can be linked to in some way below.

drench	trench	ambulance	licence	absence	finance
stench	clench	audience	silence	nuisance	entrance

1. ditch ____________________
2. water ____________________
3. money ____________________
4. hospital ____________________
5. door ____________________
6. concert ____________________
7. smell ____________________
8. noise ____________________
9. truancy ____________________
10. fist ____________________
11. pest ____________________
12. driving ____________________

Parent/Teacher Signature　　　　　　　　Date

UNIT 60

Letter patterns, sh sounds

A number of different letter groups make the **sh** sound: (a) **ci** and **ce**, as in **delicious** and **ocean** (b) **si**, as in **tension** (c) **ti** as in **action**.

A Write each word in the box in its correct sentence below.

conscious	**physician**	**admission**	**essential**
delicious	**suspicious**	**compassion**	**infectious**
ferocious	**ocean**	**extension**	**patient**
musician	**crustacean**	**dimensions**	**nutritious**

1. The black panther is a very ________________ cat.
2. The trawler scooped fish from the depths of the ________________.
3. Tom asked for an ________________ to complete his assignment.
4. The very ill ________________ was moved to another ward.
5. These people must be isolated if the disease is very ________________.
6. The general displayed ________________ for the captives.
7. The police were ________________ of the man's behaviour.
8. These oysters have a ________________ taste.
9. After being knocked out Tom is now ________________ again.
10. He consulted a ________________ about his illness.
11. Ethan made an ________________ of his guilt.
12. Oxygen is ________________ for human life to exist.
13. These nuts we grow are very ________________.
14. We measured all the ________________ of the shapes.
15. A crab and a yabby are types of ________________.
16. He is a leading ________________ in a pop band.

B Write these words in sentences of your own:

magician ________________________________

obsession ________________________________

collection ________________________________

Parent/Teacher Signature Date

Revision

A Add a pair of consonants to complete each word.

1. ____izzard (snow storm)
2. ____onze (metal)
3. ____agon (fire breathing monster)
4. ____ounder (ocean fish)
5. ____imson (red colour)
6. ____am (shellfish)
7. ____avel (small stones)
8. ____agment (piece of something)
9. ____ucose (type of sugar)
10. ____ecious (valuable)
11. ____ock (protective garment)
12. ____unk (black and white animal)

B Sort the words in the box under their correct headings below.

canary	**canoe**	**geometry**	**garment**
sponge	**guitar**	**central**	**oblige**
justice	**except**	**guest**	**common**
gallop	**barge**	**culture**	**citizen**

Soft c	Hard c	Soft g	Hard g
____	____	____	____
____	____	____	____
____	____	____	____
____	____	____	____

C Add ght, nce or nch in the spaces to complete each word.

1. drou_____ (period of dry weather)
2. reside______ (home)
3. que______ (to overcome thirst)
4. frei______ (load on a truck)
5. twili_______ (evening)
6. wre______ (type of spanner)
7. sente______ (group of words)
8. kni______ (warrior in armour)

Parent/Teacher Signature Date

Test 1

The underlined words are spelled wrongly. Write them correctly on the line.

1	The <u>night</u> swung the sword around his head.	1
2	The king lived in a large <u>casle</u>.	2
3	When she fell she injured her <u>nee</u>.	3
4	The <u>crums</u> of food were eaten by the birds.	4
5	The leaves fall from deciduous trees in <u>autum</u>.	5
6	The stallion <u>whinnyed</u> to the mares.	6
7	Don't <u>scold</u> yourself with the boiling water.	7
8	She ate the <u>staghetti</u> for tea.	8
9	He plays a <u>skarinet</u> in the school band.	9
10	A large <u>sedar</u> tree grew in the yard.	10
11	I am <u>sertain</u> he will arrive soon.	11
12	I looked up the dates on the <u>kalendar</u>.	12

Total correct ________ / 12

Parent/Teacher Signature   Date

Test 2

If the underlined word is spelled correctly place a tick on the line. If it is spelled wrongly write it correctly on the line.

1	These diamonds are jenuine.	1
2	The gard showed me where the cell was.	2
3	I ate the delicious sponge cake.	3
4	We played indoor cricket in the jymnasium.	4
5	We slept throughout the long, dark nite.	5
6	The plumbers dug a trentch for the pipes.	6
7	The new student became a serious nuisance.	7
8	The stench of the drain could be smelled all day.	8
9	He asked a fysictean to check her heartbeat.	9
10	A crab is a kind of crustacean.	10
11	Polio is an infectshus disease.	11
12	I became suspiscious of her odd behaviour.	12

Total correct ______ / 12

Parent/Teacher Signature Date

UNIT 64

Proper nouns and adjectives

A proper adjective is created by making a spelling change to a proper noun, which is the name of a person or place.

Examples: Australia, Australian; Poland, Polish; Britain, British

Write a proper adjective for each proper noun given in brackets after these sentences.

1. I ate some ________________ souvlaki. (Greece)
2. We ordered ________________ muffins for breakfast. (England)
3. I met a ________________ boy at the international fair. (Holland)
4. My uncle sometimes wears a ________________ kilt. (Scotland)
5. We ate in a ________________ café last night. (China)
6. I enjoy the taste of ________________ cheese. (Switzerland)
7. We ordered some snails in the ________________ restaurant. (France)
8. This tree usually grows only in the ________________ Region. (Alps)
9. I used a ________________ blanket to put under the saddle. (Mexico)
10. I saw a ________________ monk in the street. (Tibet)
11. The soup was made from ________________ leeks. (Wales)
12. This curry is an ________________ dish. (India)
13. He works as a detective for the ________________ mounted police. (Canada)
14. I listened to a ________________ story teller at the market. (Pakistan)
15. This dish is made with ________________ tomato paste. (Italy)
16. This old ship once served in the ________________ navy. (Portugal)

Parent/Teacher Signature Date

Sound patterns, ary

The word ending **ary** is easy to confuse with the word endings **ery** and **ory** as their pronunciation is similar.

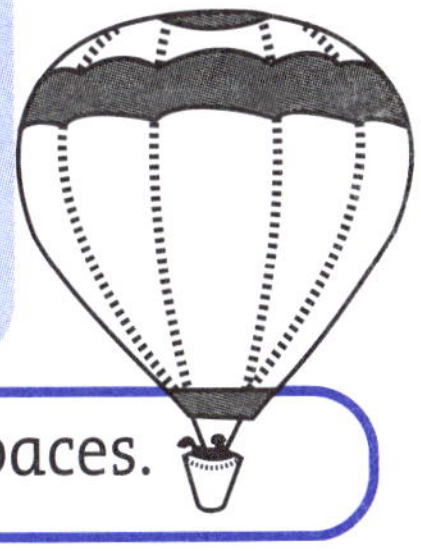

A Choose the correct word from the box to fill the spaces.

necessary	**stationary**	**boundary**	**burglary**
documentary	**granary**	**anniversary**	**salary**
missionary	**secretary**	**legendary**	**diary**
dictionary	**temporary**	**extraordinary**	**military**

1. After the ________________ many valuables are missing.
2. The umpire blew the whistle when the ball went over the ________________.
3. The train is standing ________________ on the line.
4. To become a teacher it is ________________ to obtain certain qualifications.
5. She wrote about the day's events in her ________________.
6. She receives a ________________ of over $100,000 per year.
7. I watched the ________________ about the Rocky Mountains.
8. All the cereal was stored in the ________________.
9. They are celebrating their fiftieth wedding ________________ tomorrow.
10. The feats of King Arthur are ________________ in English history.
11. An ________________ event that amazed us all occurred last night.
12. Riley, whose father is a general, also hopes to pursue a ________________ career.
13. Isabella works as ________________ to the manager.
14. The road block is only ________________.
15. A Christian ________________ was sent to the Pacific Islands in 1840.
16. We looked up the word abstemious in the ________________.

B Write these words in sentences of your own:

vocabulary ________________________________

glossary ________________________________

Parent/Teacher Signature   Date

UNIT 66

Sound patterns, ery and ory

The word endings **ery** and **ory** are also often confused as they often sound the same.

A Write each word in the box beside its meaning below.

victory	**history**	**celery**	**grocery**
artery	**auditory**	**dormitory**	**laboratory**
machinery	**mystery**	**surgery**	**memory**
observatory	**nursery**	**inventory**	**bribery**

1. record of things that happened in the past. ____________
2. a vegetable ____________
3. a blood vessel ____________
4. a shop where you can buy food items ____________
5. a large room for sleeping ____________
6. a place where babies, or plant seedlings are cared for ____________
7. a list of all the things at a certain place ____________
8. to illegally get what you want by giving people money or goods ____________
9. a place to observe the stars ____________
10. objects that do work for people ____________
11. a successful event ____________
12. to do with hearing ____________
13. a place where science experiments are carried out ____________
14. recollections ____________
15. an operation ____________
16. something odd that cannot be explained ____________

B Write these words in sentences of your own:

discovery ____________

misery ____________

compulsory ____________

Parent/Teacher Signature Date

Vowel alternations

The sounds of vowels can change when you add a suffix. This is called vowel alternation.

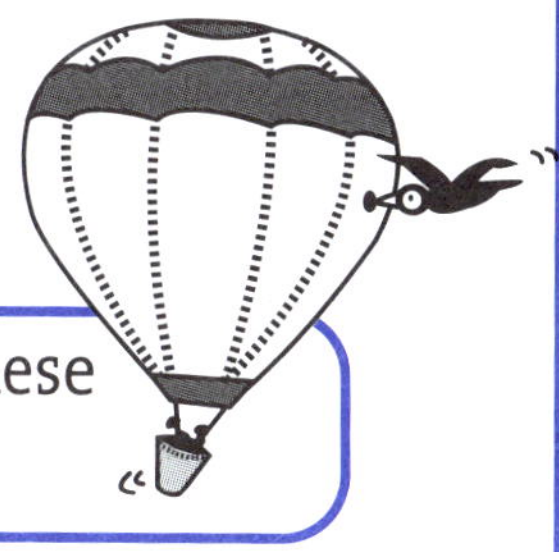

A Choose the correct word in brackets to complete these sentences.

1. We must quickly ______________ for their arrival. (prepare, preparation)
2. I believe Sam has the right ______________ for this job. (qualify, qualification)
3. We must ______________ the insects into their groups. (classify, classification)
4. We did not understand the ______________ of the situation. (grave, gravity)
5. The school's ______________ carnival was held yesterday. (athlete, athletic)
6. I do not know the correct ______________ of that word. (derive, derivation)
7. Sophie is going to ______________ the poem she learned. (recite, recitation)
8. The dictionary gave a good ______________ of the word. (define, definition)
9. I accepted their kind ______________ to the party. (invite, invitation)
10. Because of the heat I began to ______________ a lot. (perspire, perspiration)

B Write the word ending in **y** that comes from the word ending in **ation** in the brackets.
Example: simplification, simplify

1. I am going to ______________ the two numbers. (multiplication)
2. Sophie told me she will ______________ the authenticity of the letter. (verification)
3. I must ______________ them that the manager is coming. (notification)
4. I hope she will ______________ the exact sizes she needs. (specification)
5. I hope the teacher will ______________ this problem for us. (clarification)
6. Jack will ______________ for the job as supervisor. (application)
7. It is wrong for her to ______________ that one of us did it. (implication)
8. The engineers will ______________ the engine before the test flight. (modification)
9. We will need to ______________ the water before drinking it. (purification)
10. This glass will ______________ the size of the insects many times. (magnification)

Parent/Teacher Signature   Date

UNIT 68

Revision

A Add **ary**, **ery** or **ory** to complete the words.

1. confection_____ (lollies, chocolates)
2. sal_____ (person's income)
3. tempor______ (for the time being only)
4. audit______ (to do with hearing)
5. dormit______ (sleeping place)
6. art______ (blood vessel)
7. myst______ (unsolved event)
8. necess______ (needed, vital)
9. cel_____ (vegetable)
10. mem_____ (sense of recall)
11. station______ (still, not moving)
12. station______ (envelopes, writing paper)
13. bound______ (the edge of a place)
14. cemet______ (where people are buried)
15. di______ (record of daily events)
16. extraordin______ (very unusual)

B Add a proper adjective using the proper noun in brackets.

1. _______________ muffin (England)
2. _______________ bridge (Holland)
3. _______________ wine (Spain)
4. _______________ trooper (Canada)
5. _______________ cheese (Switzerland)
6. _______________ meal (Vietnam)
7. _______________ café (China)
8. _______________ soup (Japan)
9. _______________ leek (Wales)
10. _______________ beer (Germany)
11. _______________ pasta (Italy)
12. _______________ vodka (Russia)

C Choose the correct word from the pairs in the box to complete the sentences below.

revise revision	sincere sincerity	divide division	severe severity

1. Ella didn't realise the _______________ of the situation.
2. All the students had to_______________ their essays.
3. The teacher knew that Jack was_______________ in his apology.
4. That_______________ sum was really hard.

Parent/Teacher Signature Date

Test

The underlined words are spelled incorrectly. Write them correctly on the lines.

	Sentence	Answer
1	She drank some Porteguse wine.	1
2	We packed the Indien tea.	2
3	I ate some Meccican tacos.	3
4	We dug up all the Werlsh leeks.	4
5	The Russin plane crashed at the air show.	5
6	This blockade is only tempary.	6
7	My great-grandparents are buried in the cemetary.	7
8	Our team had a great victery over the others.	8
9	It is a mistary what happened to the money.	9
10	The children ate all the confectionary we gave them.	10
11	We celebrated my parents' wedding anniversory.	11
12	The scientists worked feverishly in the laboratary.	12

Total correct ______ / 12

Parent/Teacher Signature Date

UNIT 70

Parts of speech, nouns

We can make nouns, or naming words, by changing the spelling of verbs, or doing words.
Example: decide (verb), decision (noun)

A Complete these sentences by making a noun from the verb in the brackets.

1. Michelle sent Lachlan an ________________ to her party. (invite)
2. The ________________ of the children decided to play netball. (remain)
3. The shopper made a ________________ to the manager. (complain)
4. We heard the sound of ________________ coming from the room. (laugh)
5. The witness gave the police a ________________ of the thief. (describe)
6. The scientist made an interesting ________________. (discover)
7. Joseph had a lot of ________________ at the swimming carnival. (succeed)
8. The ________________ in this restaurant is very slow. (serve)
9. The football coach gave me a lot of good ________________. (advise)
10. The students' ________________ has improved this term. (behave)

B This time write the verb from which each noun in brackets has been formed.

1. The teacher asked us to ________________ our actions. (explanation)
2. My mother said she would ________________ me to leave early. (allowance)
3. I helped my brother ________________ the room. (cleanliness)
4. My parents asked me to ________________ my present. (choice)
5. The cat tried to ________________ the mouse in its claws. (seizure)
6. Grasshoppers will ________________ this cereal crop. (destruction)
7. We did not ________________ his incredible story. (belief)
8. A magpie will often ________________ the noises of others birds. (imitation)
9. We all hope our team does not ________________ today. (loss)
10. We worried that the bomb might ________________. (explosion)

Parent/Teacher Signature Date

Parts of speech, adjectives

Some describing words, or adjectives, can be formed from naming words, or nouns. The noun **winter** can become the adjective **wintry** and the noun **gold** can become the adjective **golden**.

A Form an adjective for each noun in brackets and write it in the space.

1. The ______________ boy drank six glasses of water. (thirst)
2. A ______________ monster prevented him from leaving the castle. (hair)
3. Ethan lost a ______________ coin last week. (value)
4. Thomas is a very ______________ worker. (energy)
5. The ship sank down to a ______________ grave. (water)
6. My parents like an ______________ night at the movies. (occasion)
7. It is ______________ for the bride and groom to kiss. (custom)
8. The ______________ chair was left on the verandah. (wood)

B Write describing words that can be formed from these nouns.

1. a ______________ day (sun)
2. a ______________ suggestion (sense)
3. my ______________ toy (favour)
4. a ______________ shape (triangle)
5. a ______________ apple (gold)
6. a ______________ jumper (wool)
7. an ______________ death (accident)
8. a ______________ dog (faith)

C Make describing words from the words in the box and write them in the appropriate space below.

star danger wind victory humour child expense loyalty

1. a ______________ team
2. an ______________ watch
3. a ______________ dog
4. some ______________ behaviour
5. a ______________ day
6. a ______________ play
7. a ______________ sky
8. a ______________ snake

Parent/Teacher Signature   Date

UNIT 72

American words and spelling

Although American people speak English, many of the words they use are different from the ones we use for the same things. Example: biscuit (Australian English), cookie (American English)

A Match the English words in the box with the underlined American words below and write each on the correct line.

tap	biscuit	holiday	footpath	nappy	petrol
softdrinks	autumn	caretaker	chemist	lollies	brumby

1. Have you changed the baby's diaper yet? ________________
2. I filled the car with gasoline. ________________
3. When I turned the faucet the water gushed out. ________________
4. During the fall the squirrels collected nuts. ________________
5. I love to drink sodas. ________________
6. I ate a cookie for my lunch. ________________
7. It will soon be our summer vacation. ________________
8. The janitor of our school helped me move the table. ________________
9. The car ran off the road and crossed the sidewalk. ________________
10. We bought the medicine at the drugstore. ________________
11. The children enjoyed the candy I gave them. ________________
12. The mustang was herded into the yard. ________________

B Sometimes Americans spell some words differently from us. Can you write the way we spell these words?

USA	Australia	USA	Australia
1. center	________________	5. jewelry	________________
2. bank check	________________	6. pajamas	________________
3. ax	________________	7. traveler	________________
4. gray	________________	8. centimeter	________________

Parent/Teacher Signature Date

Review

A Sort the words in the box under their headings below.

remain flask sugar wallet swamp cigar glass daisy

a = ar sound	a = short o sound	ar = ar sound	ai = long a sound

B Rewrite the sentences to make the underlined word a plural, meaning more than one.

1. After she washed the <u>dish</u> she sowed three <u>patch</u> on the jeans.

2. The three <u>fox</u> had to avoid the two speeding <u>bus</u>.

3. At the three <u>factory</u> there were more than twenty <u>trolley</u>.

4. All the <u>donkey</u> have gone into the six <u>alley</u>.

5. She covered the six <u>knife</u> with six <u>handkerchief</u>.

6. The five <u>mouse</u> had all their <u>tooth</u> extracted.

C Sort the words in the box under their headings below.

diaper	**rubbish**	**lollies**	**trash**
vacation	**holiday**	**nappy**	**candy**

Australian words		American equivalents	

Parent/Teacher Signature Date

Test 1

Circle the one word in each sentence that is spelled wrongly and write it correctly on the line.

1	There was a large humpback whail in the water.	1
2	The curtin was hung over the window.	2
3	Ella is a very polyte person.	3
4	We viewed the stars through the teleskope.	4
5	Cooper filled the bottel with water.	5
6	There are several tiny inseks in the jar.	6
7	Sarah took her umberella because it looked like rain.	7
8	We saw lots of donkies on the farm.	8
9	There are several volcanos erupting right now.	9
10	The camel walked across the dessert.	10
11	The dog tried to berry the bone in the lawn.	11
12	Her voyce sounds quite hoarse.	12

Total correct ________
12

Parent/Teacher Signature Date

Test 2

Choose the correct spelling of each word from the brackets and write it on the line.

1	In the garden grew lots of (thisles, thistles).	1
2	He missed the nail and hit his (thum, thumb)	2
3	There is a large (castle, cassel) on the hill.	3
4	The knight raised his (sord, sword) above his head.	4
5	We (often, offen) go to the movies.	5
6	Did you give the teacher the correct (answer, anser)?	6
7	A large (parm, palm) tree grew in the backyard.	7
8	There was no (dout, doubt) who had done it.	8
9	She cut her finger with the (nife, knife).	9
10	We could hear the (eko, echo) in the hills.	10
11	I (new, knew) my answer would be right.	11
12	I wrote on the board with (chork, chalk).	12

Total correct ________
12

Parent/Teacher Signature Date

Test 3

Choose the correct spelling of each word in the brackets and write it on the line.

1 Smoking is (band, banned) in this café. 1

2 Mike nearly (guessed, guest) the correct answer. 2

3 There was a (miner, minor) accident at the corner. 3

4 What (root, route) are you taking to Canberra. 4

5 The (peddle, pedal) on the bike became loose. 5

6 Some (hair, hare) is falling out of my head. 6

7 It took me a (hole, whole) hour to finish. 7

8 She pushed her foot on the (brake, break) pedal. 8

9 I became (bored, board) during the long speech. 9

10 The boards in this old house (creek, creak) a lot. 10

11 I picked a beautiful red (rose, rows) in the garden. 11

12 These shoes are going (cheeply, cheaply). 12

Total correct ______ / 12

Parent/Teacher Signature Date

Useful Words

The following list, developed by teachers over many years, includes words that students at this level should be aware of and be able to spell. If a student is progressing at a satisfactory level of vocabulary development, these words should be understood.

aboard
action
addition
address
afraid
allow
although
amount
answer
appear
appoint
arrest
attempt
attend
August
automobile
await
awful
beautiful
beg
between
board
carried
chief
cities
claim
clerk
comfort
command
company
complaint
connection
contain
convict
crowd
daughter
debate
declare
degree
department

desire
destroy
direct
direction
district
does
don't
due
during
duty
effort
eight
either
elect
election
empire
employ
enclose
engage
engine
enjoy
enough
entire
entrance
escape
estate
everything
fact
factory
family
famous
favour
field
fifth
figure
final
firm
flight
form
fortune

forty
forward
fourth
friend
further
gentleman
guest
holiday
human
importance
important
include
information
instead
intend
jail
judge
justice
knew
known
ledge
length
liberty
listen
loss
madam
mayor
measure
Mrs
navy
nearly
newspaper
none
o'clock
objection
oblige
obtain
perfect
period
personal

pleasure
police
population
position
present
president
primary
prison
private
progress
prompt
proper
property
public
publish
pyjamas
quite
raise
rapid
rate
rather
refuse
regard
region
relative
remain
remember
repair
reply
represent
request
restrain
result
retire
royal
running
sail
Saturday
second
section

select
September
serve
setting
several
shed
since
slide
sometimes
special
spend
station
struck
sudden
suppose
surprise
terrible
themselves
though
through
throw
Thursday
travel
trouble
truly
Tuesday
uncle
until
usual
view
visit
wait
weather
which
whole
whom
whose
women
wonderful
worth

WINK: Words I Need to Know

For many people, some words are often problematic to spell. Record words you are having difficulty with on this page.

Word	Word	Word

Some Tips for Learning to Spell

- ★ When you read, look out for the patterns of letters you find in words. Remembering these will help you spell words. For example, these words do not sound the same, but all contain a common letter pattern: cough, rough, through, thought, bough.
- ★ Take an interest in words, as this is useful in motivating you to persevere with improving your spelling ability.
- ★ Accept that some difficult words simply have to be learned. A useful strategy for this is the LOOK, COVER, WRITE, CHECK system.

    LOOK at the word and try to form a pattern of the letters in your mind. Ensure you know the meaning of the word and how it is used.

    COVER the word or remove it from your sight.

    WRITE the word from memory.

    CHECK if you are correct.

  If wrong, begin the process again. If right, give yourself a pat on the back.
- ★ Learn to say words correctly. Many students often have spelling difficulties simply because they pronounce some words incorrectly, and spell them as they think they sound. For example: jumping, not jumpen.
- ★ Develop the dictionary habit. If you don't know how to spell a word, look it up. Did you know a dictionary is used more for finding the correct spelling of words rather than finding their meanings?
- ★ Become familiar with the more common rules and guides, and use them.
- ★ When you are writing and you have guessed the spelling of a word, always check it later.
- ★ Remember that incorrect spelling is easily noticed by others, so being a good speller can be an aid to employment.

Assessment

	T1	T2	T3	T4
★ Reads widely and takes an interest in words and their meanings.				
★ Is prepared to make informed attempts at spelling.				
★ Spells at a standard commensurate with his or her age.				
★ Uses a variety of methods to improve spelling skills, such as sounds and patterns.				
★ Takes care to review and proofread own writing attempts.				
★ Readily identifies errors in proofreading activities.				
★ Continually displays a determination and desire to improve spelling.				
★ Is aware that words that sound the same may have different spellings.				
★ Makes correct vowel alternation from long to short vowels.				

Comments

Teacher

____

____

Student

____

____

Glossary of Terms

adjective
A *word* that describes *nouns* or other words.
Examples: **gold** (noun), **golden** (adjective)
wool (noun), **woollen** (adjective)

American word usage
Although Americans speak English like Australians do, many of the words they commonly use differ from Australian word usage. Examples: Australians say **footpath** but Americans say **sidewalk**.
Australians say **rubbish** but Americans say **trash**.

anagram
A *word* or words that contains exactly the same letters but in a different order.
Examples: **pea**, **ape**; **fowl**, **flow**, **wolf**; **seaside**, **disease**

comparative
An *adjective* that shows a degree of comparison between two or more things.
Examples: **big** (one), **bigger** (two), **biggest** (three or more); Jack is tall but Tom is taller.

complex consonant group
A consonant unit (**ch**, **ck**, **dge**, **tch**) occurring at the end of a *word*, determined by the preceding *vowel* sound. Examples: **tch** follows a short vowel sound, as in **catch**, **fetch**, **itch**, **crutch**; **ch** follows a long vowel sound, as in **beach** and **coach**

compound word
A *word* made up of two or more smaller words, often developing first as a hyphenated word.
Examples: **butter** + **fly** = **butterfly**;

consonant
A letter in which the air is in some way impeded when pronounced. There are 21 consonants in the alphabet, all the letters that are not *vowels*.

consonant blend
When two or more *consonants* come together to blend a sound. Examples: **stick**, **sky**, **brown**, **straw**. Consonant blends may be initial blends (**frog**), medial (middle) blends (**blister**), or final blends (**stamp**).

contraction
A *word* in which one or more letters have been omitted and in their place an apostrophe inserted.
Examples: **I would** becomes **I'd**; **is not** becomes **isn't**

digraph
A combination of letters that represents a single sound. There are *consonant* digraphs and *vowel* digraphs. Common consonant digraphs include **sh**, **ch**, **th** and **wh**. (Consonant digraphs at the beginning of a word are called an onset.) A vowel digraph is called a *diphthong*.

homograph
A *word* that is spelled the same as another word, but each word is pronounced differently and has a different meaning (a type of homonym). Examples: **desert** (dry barren area) and **desert** (abandon); **close** (near) and **close** (shut)

homonym
A *word* that is spelled and/or pronounced the same as another word but each word has a different meaning. *Homographs* and *homophones* are both types of homonym, and some homonyms are both homographs and homophones. Examples: **tear** (rip) and **tear** (result of crying); **fair** (blond) and **fare** (cost of a train ticket); **bank** (place to exchange money) and **bank** (either side of a river)

homophone
A *word* that is pronounced the same as another word, but each word has a different spelling and a different meaning. Examples: **bear** (a furry animal) and **bare** (naked);
sure (certain) and **shore** (coastline)

letter pattern
A letter sequence that functions as a unit and is related to a consistent category of sound.
Example: **one** = **bone**, **cone**, **tone**

long vowel
The sound of a *vowel* (**a**, **e**, **i**, **o**, **u**) that says its letter name, or is an *r-influenced vowel*.
Examples: **same**, **bacon**, **far**, **concrete**, **fever**, **fine**, **rival**, **fir**, **cone**, **robot**, **core**, **cute**, **student**, **purr**

noun
A *word* that refers to the names of everything around us.

phonics
The systematic relationship between letters and sounds.

phonogram
One of a group of words that end in a common rhyme and that vary only in the beginning consonant. Examples: **back, hack, lack, sack, tack**

plural
More than one. Most words make their plurals by adding an s. However, there are other ways to make the plurals of words. Examples: **girl, girls; watch, watches; city, cities; piano, pianos; knife, knives; tooth, teeth; mouse, mice**

portmanteau word
A *word* created by joining a part of one word to a part of another. They were first created by Lewis Carroll, who wrote *Alice in Wonderland.*
Examples: **brunch** from breakfast and lunch; **smog** from smoke and fog

possessive
A *word* that shows that someone (or something) has ownership through the use of an apostrophe.
Example: **the boy's bike; the ladies' dresses**

prefix
Letters added to the beginning of a *word*, sometimes to make its opposite. We simply add these and no spelling changes to the base word are necessary.
Example: **in + visible = invisible**

proper adjective
An adjective formed from a proper noun.

Examples: **England** (noun), **English** (adjective); **China** (noun) **Chinese** (adjective)

proper noun
A *word* that refers to a particular person, place or thing. Examples: **Paul, Canada, Murray River**

r-influenced vowel
A vowel sound that is determined by the letter r following it. Example: the a in **far** is a *long vowel* sound but the a in **fad** is a *short vowel* sound.

root word
A *word* or word part that has its origin in Old English, Latin or Greek and that provides the basis of many other words. Example: **aero** (air) = **aerial, aeroplane, aerobics**

short vowel
The sound of a *vowel* (a, e, i, o and u) that is clipped — a short sound. It is sometimes said short vowel sounds are the "baby" sounds.
Examples: **bat, bet, bit, bottle, but**

shortened word
A word that, over the years, has become shortened.
Example: **omnibus** (full version in use fifty or more years ago), **bus** (current usage)

silent (unsounded) letter
A letter in some words that is not pronounced but is still included in the word.
Examples: **lamb, know, pneumonia, sword, wrap**

suffix
A *word* ending that alters the word's part of speech (noun to adjective, for example) or meaning. Spelling changes are often needed.
Example: **beauty + ful = beautiful**

syllable
A sound unit that includes only one sounded *vowel.* The vowel may be preceded or followed by several *consonants.* Words can be divided into their syllables. This is a useful spelling technique.
Example: **development = de / vel / op / ment**

vowel
A letter in which the air passes through the mouth without obstruction when pronounced. The letters a, e, i, o and u are vowels. Note: y does the work of the vowels i and e in words such as **cry** (long i), **mystery** (short i) and **weary** (long e).

vowel alternation
The process by which the pronunciation of a *vowel* changes in the base word while the spelling does not change.

Example: the long-to-short vowel change in the related words **crime** and **criminal**

word
A unit of meaning. A word may be a simple *syllable* or a combination of syllables. A word may contain smaller units of meaning within it.

Answers, Book 5

Unit 1

A

1. lamb
2. gnat
3. camel
4. apple
5. dragon
6. dam
7. taxi
8. flash
9. mat

B

1. crane
2. chase
3. strange
4. paste
5. stable
6. exhale
7. oasis
8. whale

C

a = ar sound: brass, flask, telecast, koala

a = short o sound: swamp, squash, swallow, quarrel

Unit 2

A

1. dress
2. dentist
3. fresh
4. rent
5. fence
6. insect
7. cent
8. scent
9. flesh
10. shed
11. seven
12. level

B

1. sincere
2. atmosphere
3. stampede
4. complete
5. severe
6. recede
7. concrete
8. sphere
9. athlete
10. serene

Unit 3

A

1. thistle
2. sister
3. litter
4. hospital
5. comic
6. prison
7. tickle
8. liquid
9. picnic
10. limb

B

1. spider
2. science
3. polite
4. mobile
5. hostile
6. hive
7. fragile
8. stride
9. wine
10. require
11. fertile
12. vampire

Unit 4

A

1. lollipop
2. continent
3. foxes
4. bottle
5. wombat
6. broth
7. shock
8. compost

B

1. doze
2. cone
3. stone
4. throne
5. frozen
6. hotel
7. toe
8. hose

C

o = short o sound: lodge, content

o = long o sound: cove, lonely

o = short u sound: among, sponge

Unit 5

A

1. crumb
2. trunk
3. slum
4. sunrise
5. uncle
6. adult
7. umbrella
8. drudge
9. ugly
10. hundred
11. under
12. skunk

B

1. moisture
2. confuse
3. furniture
4. duel
5. pupil
6. population
7. amuse
8. secure
9. future
10. bugle
11. puncture
12. perfume

Unit 6

A

1. sugar
2. cigar
3. depart
4. carpet
5. carve
6. burglar
7. vinegar
8. orchard
9. marble
10. separate

B

1. container
2. faithful
3. bait
4. hurray
5. straight
6. quail
7. tray
8. daisy
9. play
10. rainbow
11. holiday
12. remain

Unit 7 Revision

A

Short a sound: elastic, taxi, animal, gravel, dragon, bandit

Long a sound: brake, debate, tasty, bacon, apricot, exhale

B

Short e sound: vent, fetch, ledge, swept

Long e sound: female, athlete, compete, concrete

Short i sound: invert, knit, until, skill

Long i sound: polite, whine, shrine, brine

C

1. subway
2. waist
3. cargo
4. prayed
5. quail
6. cardigan

Unit 8 Test 1

1. camel
2. marble
3. faithful
4. skunk
5. perfume
6. bugle
7. spider
8. bottle
9. hotel
10. telescope
11. concrete
12. hospital

Unit 9 Test 2

1. whale
2. canal
3. swallow
4. dentist
5. athlete
6. picnic
7. science
8. money
9. frozen
10. umbrella
11. puncture
12. burglar

Unit 10

1. houses
2. patches
3. dishes
4. pencils
5. witches
6. crashes
7. dresses
8. buses
9. lashes
10. boxes
11. punches
12. classes
13. kisses
14. beaches
15. speeches
16. catches

Unit 11

1. lollies
2. fillies
3. alleys
4. donkeys
5. jockeys
6. jellies
7. flies
8. worries
9. trolleys
10. pathways
11. valleys
12. holidays
13. chimneys
14. salaries
15. diaries
16. factories

Unit 12

1. dwarfs
2. giraffes
3. scarves
4. potatoes
5. heroes
6. loaves
7. halves
8. wolves
9. handkerchiefs
10. pianos
11. themselves
12. knives
13. lives
14. echoes
15. tornadoes
16. shelves

Unit 13

1. deer
2. trousers
3. children
4. mice
5. teeth
6. trout
7. gallows
8. bellows
9. scissors
10. women
11. cattle
12. feet
13. species
14. spectacles
15. lice
16. geese

Unit 14 Revision

A

1. jelly, jellies
2. engine, engines
3. stitch, stitches
4. monkey, monkeys
5. kidney, kidneys
6. echo, echoes
7. fly, flies
8. loaf, loaves
9. body, bodies
10. foot, feet

B

1. mice
2. storeys
3. wives
4. berries
5. kisses
6. saucers
7. matches
8. buses
9. cities
10. knives

Unit 15 Test

1. pencils
2. kisses
3. diaries
4. factories
5. jockeys
6. mice
7. knives
8. shelves
9. pianos
10. tomatoes
11. storeys
12. matches

Unit 16

1. banned
2. dessert
3. current
4. serial
5. sauce
6. lightning
7. guest
8. higher
9. hire
10. band
11. lightening
12. desert
13. currant
14. source
15. guessed
16. cereal

Unit 17

1. pedal
2. hangar
3. route
4. bury
5. night
6. boarder
7. censor
8. minor
9. miner
10. border
11. knight
12. root
13. berry
14. hanger
15. peddle
16. sensor

Unit 18

1. magnifying
2. current
3. erratic
4. audience
5. altar
6. missile
7. operation
8. primary
9. astronomer
10. autograph
11. electricity
12. hydrant
13. cosmetics
14. pedals
15. legends
16. fort or fortress
17. homestead
18. engraved

Unit 19

A

1. applause
2. automatic
3. autumn
4. exhaust
5. taut
6. fraud
7. saucer
8. sausage
9. auction
10. cauliflower

B

1. flaw
2. drawl
3. outlaw
4. sprawled
5. awkward
6. gnaw
7. trawler
8. strawberries
9. scrawl
10. awesome

Unit 20

A

1. disease
2. teachers
3. season
4. grease
5. bleach
6. breathe
7. treaty
8. beak
9. squeak
10. peaceful

B

1. weapon
2. jealous
3. heavy
4. break
5. death
6. steak
7. weather
8. sweat
9. head
10. dread

Unit 21

A

1. succeed
2. canteen
3. screech
4. keel
5. breeze
6. cheerful
7. steeple
8. referee
9. toffee
10. leech
11. heed
12. sneeze

B

1. loathe
2. loaves
3. moat
4. coax
5. foam
6. approach
7. cocoa
8. boastful
9. cloak
10. soaking
11. toadstool
12. hoax

Unit 22

A

1. schooner
2. kangaroo
3. stoop
4. hooligan
5. noose
6. bamboo
7. cockatoo
8. oozing
9. choosing
10. cartoon
11. igloo
12. lagoon

B

1. boil
2. noisy
3. disappoint
4. rejoice
5. moisture
6. appoint
7. poise
8. poisonous
9. quoit
10. voice
11. ointment
12. coin

Unit 23

A

1. hornet
2. scorch
3. enormous
4. gorgeous
5. absorb
6. tornado
7. porch
8. north
9. organ
10. morsel
11. sword
12. orchard

B

1. drowsy
2. town
3. rowdy
4. coward
5. powder
6. vowel
7. trowel
8. eyebrows
9. renown
10. jowls

C

1. burrow
2. rainbow
3. elbow
4. shallow
5. sparrow

Unit 24

A

ou = ow sound: flounder, hound, devour, astound
ou = long oo sound: youth, soup, group, you
ou = short u sound: double, cousin, trouble, touch

B

1. absurd
2. turnip
3. furniture
4. hamburger
5. surgeon
6. purchase
7. urgent
8. burden
9. suburb
10. turkey
11. murder
12. sunburn

Unit 25 Revision

A

1. squeak
2. cauliflower
3. scrawl
4. teacher
5. flaw
6. sausage
7. season
8. claw
9. taut
10. outlaw
11. auction
12. dread

B

1. sparrow
2. morsel
3. flounder
4. soup
5. elbow
6. absorb
7. north
8. shallow
9. hound
10. touch
11. burrow
12. acorn

C

1. turkey
2. cousin
3. steeple
4. coward
5. hoax
6. hornet
7. drowsy
8. surgeon
9. loathe
10. powder
11. moisture
12. bamboo

Unit 26 Test 1

1. auction
2. strawberries
3. cauliflowers
4. teacher
5. dreamed
6. weather
7. succeed
8. referee
9. loaves
10. sneeze
11. sweat
12. breakfast

Unit 27 Test 2

1. surgeon
2. automatic
3. awkward
4. turkey
5. soup
6. furniture
7. vowels
8. enormous
9. drowsy
10. cockatoo
11. poisonous
12. referee

Unit 28

A

1. action
2. affection
3. subtraction
4. prediction
5. extinction
6. impression
7. profession
8. expression
9. selection
10. distinction

B

1. congratulations
2. imitation
3. complications
4. decorations
5. education
6. separation
7. production
8. introduction
9. creation
10. reduction

Unit 29

A

1. permission
2. erosion
3. collision
4. explosion
5. transmission
6. conclusion
7. inspiration
8. opposition
9. examination
10. definition

B

1. discussion
2. contraction
3. generation
4. imitation
5. complication
6. persuasion
7. exploration
8. combination

Unit 30

A

1. perishable
2. dependable
3. profitable
4. remarkable
5. expendable
6. laughable
7. visible
8. audible
9. edible

10. legible
11. possible
12. terrible

B

1. changeable
2. desirable
3. lovable
4. deplorable
5. peaceable
6. serviceable
7. noticeable
8. usable
9. presumable
10. comparable
11. manageable
12. excusable

Unit 31

A

1. brushed
2. wasted
3. described
4. denied
5. dripped
6. hurried
7. replied
8. buried
9. travelled
10. stirred
11. knitted
12. stopped

B

1. studied
2. captured
3. copied
4. explored
5. celebrated
6. continued
7. chopped
8. preferred
9. shopped
10. relaxed
11. chased
12. qualified

Unit 32 Revision

A

1. agreeable
2. affordable
3. punishable
4. profitable
5. expandable

B

1. comfortable
2. legible
3. combustible
4. credible
5. remarkable
6. predictable
7. reliable
8. navigable
9. valuable
10. respectable
11. refillable
12. horrible

C

1. described
2. studied
3. chopped
4. continued
5. buried
6. travelled
7. brushed
8. hugged
9. replied
10. stirred
11. dripped
12. celebrated

Unit 33 Test

1. punishable
2. horrible
3. combustible
4. buried
5. travelled
6. permission
7. conclusion
8. impression
9. education
10. decoration
11. affection
12. explosion

Unit 34

A

1. haystack
2. crossroads
3. earthquake
4. elsewhere
5. pipeline
6. sunglasses
7. downstairs
8. horseback
9. lookout
10. fingerprint
11. signwriter
12. starlight

B

1. backyard
2. seagull
3. lifejackets
4. headphones
5. campfire
6. lifesavers
7. roadworks
8. overboard
9. landfill
10. barefoot
11. landmark
12. fireproof

Unit 35

A

1. gorilla
2. accelerate
3. rabbit
4. alligator
5. mannequin
6. hurricane
7. corridor
8. mammoth
9. daffodil
10. moccasin
11. jewellery
12. mayonnaise

B

1. buzzard
2. abattoir
3. mutton
4. professor
5. hippotamus
6. blizzard
7. squirrel
8. passenger
9. sapphire
10. innocent
11. porridge
12. antenna

C

1. puffin
2. cheddar
3. broccoli
4. saddle
5. exaggerate
6. attic

Unit 36

A

1. flame + glare
2. breakfast + lunch
3. motor + pedal
4. motor + hotel
5. smoke + fog
6. medical + care
7. breath + analyser
8. helicopter + port
9. news + broadcast
10 television + broadcast

B

1. paratroopers
2. glimmer
3. twirl
4. motorcade
5. melodrama
6. never
7. squiggle
8. hi-fi
9. autobank
10. smash

Unit 37

A

1. cutlery
2. machinery
3. perspire
4. nursery
5. certain
6. camera
7. modern
8. whispered
9. liberty
10. battery

B

1. fever
2. miserable
3. saucer
4. litter
5. answered
6. laughter
7. passenger
8. stationery
9. revolver
10. interfere
11. verse
12. rhinoceros

Unit 38

A

1. flask
2. calm
3. fast
4. palm
5. mast
6. banana
7. glass
8. calf
9. koala
10. basket

B

1. waratah
2. squadron
3. washer
4. quarry
5. watched
6. squash

7. wallet
8. wallaby
9. quantity
10. quarrel
11. swamp
12. swan

Unit 39

1. chemist
2. chapel
3. chaplain
4. quench
5. charity
6. chemical
7. chaos
8. champagne
9. machine
10. parachute
11. chaff
12. cherry

B

1. watch
2. latch
3. bitch
4. witch
5. satchel
6. catch
7. stretch
8. britches
9. match
10. itch
11. batch
12. kitchen

Unit 40

A

1. python
2. cyclone
3. nylon
4. hyphen
5. hydrant
6. hygienic
7. flyer
8. dyeing
9. clarify
10. rhyming
11. magnify
12. multiply

B

1. empty
2. poultry
3. guilty
4. easily
5. laundry
6. mystery
7. luckily
8. rapidly

9. any
10. pansy
11. platypus
12. safety

Unit 41

A

1. edge
2. knowledge
3. fudge
4. porridge
5. badge
6. hedge
7. dodge
8. ledge
9. judge
10. gadget

B

1. chuckle
2. quickly
3. stocking
4. jacket
5. wicked
6. buckle
7. hockey
8. cockatoo
9. paddock
10. locker
11. wicket
12. locket

Unit 42

A

1. faithful
2. thistles
3. theology
4. eighth
5. author
6. thermal
7. thumb
8. therefore
9. leather
10. marathon
11. warmth
12. feather

B

1. accomplish
2. extinguish
3. perish
4. marsh
5. demolish
6. astonish
7. shriek
8. mushroom
9. vanish
10. bishop

Unit 43 Revision

A

y = long i sound: flyer, cyclone, nylon, python, hyphen, hygiene
y = long e sound: empty, guilty, pansy
y = short i sound: mysterious, physical, platypus

B

1. vanish
2. jacket
3. author
4. wicked
5. mushroom
6. marathon
7. warmth
8. finished
9. faithful
10. hockey
11. cushion
12. buckle

C

a = ar sound: palm, fast, calf, basket, glass, flask
a = short o sound: swan, wattle, quarrel, wallaby, quarry, watch

Unit 44 Test 1

1. machinery
2. rhinoceros
3. verses
4. koala
5. wallet
6. quarrel
7. parachute
8. kitchen
9. machine
10. quench
11. calm
12. quarry

Unit 45 Test 2

1. knowledge
2. wickets
3. extinguish
4. mushroom
5. faithful
6. dyeing
7. cyclone
8. hyphen
9. easily
10. safety
11. nylon
12. locket

Unit 46

A

1. winning
2. shrinking
3. walking
4. rushing
5. catching
6. getting
7. chopping
8. shopping
9. planting
10. panning
11. begging
12. mending
13. skipping
14. thinning
15. swimming
16. flapping

B

1. tearing
2. wrapping

Unit 47

A

1. coming
2. damaging
3. chasing
4. separating
5. queueing
6. purchasing
7. canoeing
8. seeing
9. forcing
10. biting
11. hoping
12. sharing
13. firing
14. diving
15. shining
16. using

B

1. taking
2. weaving

Unit 48

A

1. inland
2. midday
3. postpone
4. unpopular
5. antidote
6. emigrate
7. outlaw
8. telescope
9. remount
10. transplant

B

1. impossible
2. unnecessary
3. disappear
4. illegal
5. illegible
6. disappoint
7. unsure
8. impolite
9. untie
10. illiterate
11. discount
12. impatient

Unit 49

A

1. misbehave
2. inexpensive
3. uniform
4. nonsense
5. uncertain
6. express
7. disappeared
8. precautions
9. triathlon
10. recapture

B

1. undress
2. dislike
3. disallow
4. unequal
5. incomplete
6. unpopular
7. unarmed
8. mislead

C

1. untrue
2. impolite
3. invisible
4. disagree
5. unhappy
6. nonsense
7. dishonest

Unit 50 Revision

A

No change: shrinking, walking, catching, rushing
Double last letter: getting, shopping, skipping, panning
Drop e: separating, purchasing, diving, chasing

B

1. misjudged
2. reheat
3. rewrite
4. unwrap
5. disregarded
6. income
7. incomplete
8. non-smoking
9. preschool
10. submarine

Unit 51 Test

1. misconduct
2. explode
3. universally
4. encourage
5. forecaster
6. misspell
7. prehistoric
8. disobeyed
9. discontented
10. nonprofit
11. forehead
12. endanger

Unit 52

A

1. you + are
2. I + have
3. you + had
4. must + not
5. did + not
6. do + not
7. was + not
8. could + not
9. had + not
10. would + not

B

1. won't
2. shouldn't
3. they'd
4. you're
5. it's
6. haven't
7. don't
8. you'll
9. haven't
10. weren't

Unit 53

1. off
2. accept
3. They're
4. cheque
5. adapt
6. illegible
7. quite
8. borne
9. dessert
10. eminent
11. defective
12. besides
13. canvas
14. chose
15. disease
16. leant

Unit 54

1. spider
2. raccoon
3. poodle
4. porcupine
5. octopus
6. orangutan
7. crocodile
8. dinosaur
9. duck
10. flamingo
11. leopard
12. caterpillar

Unit 55

A

1. lamb
2. debt
3. thistle
4. castle
5. doubt
6. knock
7. thumb
8. Wednesday
9. hymn
10. often
11. scissors
12. knife

B

1. wrong
2. school
3. sword
4. palm
5. calf
6. beret
7. yolk
8. knee

C

1. hour
2. knuckle
3. comb
4. dinghy
5. plumber
6. chemist
7. scent
8. knob or knocker

Unit 56

A

1. smirk
2. scarlet
3. professor
4. gradual
5. fragile
6. platypus
7. crayon
8. drought
9. skull
10. florist
11. stallion
12. clarinet

B

1. scald
2. granite
3. fragrant
4. trombone
5. glutton
6. spinach
7. skeleton
8. flamingo
9. twinkle
10. spaghetti
11. proverb
12. snorkel

Unit 57

A

1. celery
2. deceive
3. cedar
4. certain
5. cigarette
6. voice
7. twice
8. medicine
9. justice
10. palace
11. cyclone
12. rhinoceros

B

1. compass
2. colony
3. canteen
4. cottage
5. carnival
6. canary
7. correct
8. country
9. calendar
10. carol

Unit 58

1. giant
2. lounge

3. genuine
4. galaxy
5. general
6. engine
7. garlic
8. groan
9. guard
10. guitar
11. guide
12. revenge
13. gymnasium
14. sponge
15. guarantee
16. government

Unit 59

A

1. delight
2. copyright
3. thought
4. insight
5. distraught
6. brought
7. caught
8. drought
9. sought
10. midnight

B

1. trench
2. drench
3. finance
4. ambulance
5. entrance
6. audience
7. stench
8. silence
9. absence
10. clench
11. nuisance
12. licence

Unit 60

A

1. ferocious
2. ocean
3. extension
4. patient
5. infectious
6. compassion
7. suspicious
8. delicious
9. conscious
10. physician
11. admission
12. essential
13. nutritious
14. dimensions
15. crustacean
16. musician

Unit 61 Revision

A

1. blizzard
2. bronze
3. dragon
4. flounder
5. crimson
6. clam
7. gravel
8. fragment
9. glucose
10. precious
11. smock
12. skunk

B

Soft c: justice, except, central, citizen

Hard c: canary, canoe, culture, common

Soft g: sponge, barge, geometry, oblige

Hard g: gallop, guitar, guest, garment

C

1. drought
2. residence
3. quench
4. freight
5. twilight
6. wrench
7. sentence
8. knight

Unit 62 Test 1

1. knight
2. castle
3. knee
4. crumbs
5. autumn
6. whinnied
7. scald
8. spaghetti
9. clarinet
10. cedar
11. certain
12. calendar

Unit 63 Test 2

1. genuine
2. guard
3. sponge ✓
4. gymnasium
5. night
6. trench
7. nuisance ✓
8. stench ✓
9. physician
10. crustacean ✓
11. infectious
12. suspicious

Unit 64

1. Greek
2. English
3. Dutch
4. Scottish
5. Chinese
6. Swiss
7. French
8. Alpine
9. Mexican
10. Tibetan
11. Welsh
12. Indian
13. Canadian
14. Pakistani
15. Italian
16. Portuguese

Unit 65

A

1. burglary
2. boundary
3. stationary
4. necessary
5. diary
6. salary
7. documentary
8. granary
9. anniversary
10. legendary
11. extraordinary
12. military
13. secretary
14. temporary
15. missionary
16. dictionary

Unit 66

A

1. history
2. celery
3. artery
4. grocery
5. dormitory
6. nursery
7. inventory
8. bribery
9. observatory
10. machinery
11. victory
12. auditory
13. laboratory
14. memory
15. surgery
16. mystery

Unit 67

A

1. prepare
2. qualification
3. classify
4. gravity
5. athletic
6. derivation
7. recite
8. definition
9. invitation
10. perspire

B

1. multiply
2. verify
3. notify
4. specify
5. clarify
6. apply
7. imply
8. modify
9. purify
10. magnify

Unit 68 Revision

A

1. confectionery
2. salary
3. temporary
4. auditory
5. dormitory
6. artery
7. mystery
8. necessary
9. celery
10. memory
11. stationary
12. stationery
13. boundary
14. cemetery
15. diary
16. extraordinary

B

1. English
2. Dutch
3. Spanish
4. Canadian
5. Swiss
6. Vietnamese
7. Chinese
8. Japanese

9. Welsh
10. German
11. Italian
12. Russian

C

1. severity
2. revise
3. sincere
4. division

Unit 69 Test

1. Portuguese
2. Indian
3. Mexican
4. Welsh
5. Russian
6. temporary
7. cemetery
8. victory
9. mystery
10. confectionery
11. anniversary
12. laboratory

Unit 70

A

1. invitation
2. remainder
3. complaint
4. laughter
5. description
6. discovery
7. success
8. service
9. advice
10. behaviour

B

1. explain
2. allow
3. clean
4. choose
5. seize
6. destroy
7. believe
8. imitate
9. lose
10. explode

Unit 71

A

1. thirsty
2. hairy
3. valuable
4. energetic
5. watery
6. occasional
7. customary
8. wooden

B

1. sunny
2. sensible
3. favourite
4. triangular
5. golden
6. woollen
7. accidental
8. faithful

C

1. victorious
2. expensive
3. loyal
4. childish
5. windy
6. humorous
7. starry
8. dangerous

Unit 72

A

1. nappy
2. petrol
3. tap
4. autumn
5. softdrinks
6. biscuit
7. holiday
8. caretaker
9. footpath
10. chemist
11. lollies
12. brumby

B

centre
cheque
axe
grey
jewellery
pyjamas
traveller
centimetre

Unit 73 Review

A

a = ar sound: flask, glass
a = short o sound: swamp, wallet
ar = ar sound: cigar, sugar
ai = long a sound: remain, daisy

B

1. After she washed the dishes she sewed three patches on the jeans.
2. The three foxes had to avoid the two speeding buses.
3. At the three factories there were more than twenty trolleys.
4. All the donkeys have gone into the six alleys.
5. She covered the six knives with six handkerchiefs.
6. The five mice had all their teeth extracted.

C

Australian: rubbish, holiday, lollies, nappy
American: diaper, vacation, trash, candy

Unit 74 Test 1

1. whale
2. curtain
3. polite
4. telescope
5. bottle
6. insects
7. umbrella
8. donkeys
9. volcanoes
10. desert
11. bury
12. voice

Unit 75 Test 2

1. thistles
2. thumb
3. castle
4. sword
5. often
6. answer
7. palm
8. doubt
9. knife
10. echo
11. knew
12. chalk

Unit 76 Test 3

1. banned
2. guessed
3. minor
4. route
5. pedal
6. hair
7. whole
8. brake
9. bored
10. creak
11. rose
12. cheaply